Garden Construction

Other Publications:

THE SEAFARERS

THE ENCYCLOPEDIA OF COLLECTIBLES

WORLD WAR II

THE GREAT CITIES

HOME REPAIR AND IMPROVEMENT

THE WORLD'S WILD PLACES

THE TIME-LIFE LIBRARY OF BOATING

HUMAN BEHAVIOR

THE ART OF SEWING

THE OLD WEST

THE EMERGENCE OF MAN

THE AMERICAN WILDERNESS

LIFE LIBRARY OF PHOTOGRAPHY

THIS FABULOUS CENTURY

FOODS OF THE WORLD

TIME-LIFE LIBRARY OF AMERICA

TIME-LIFE LIBRARY OF ART

GREAT AGES OF MAN

LIFE SCIENCE LIBRARY

THE LIFE HISTORY OF THE UNITED STATES

TIME READING PROGRAM

LIFE NATURE LIBRARY

LIFE WORLD LIBRARY

FAMILY LIBRARY:
    HOW THINGS WORK IN YOUR HOME
    THE TIME-LIFE BOOK OF THE FAMILY CAR
    THE TIME-LIFE FAMILY LEGAL GUIDE
    THE TIME-LIFE BOOK OF FAMILY FINANCE

Garden Construction

by
OGDEN TANNER
and
the Editors of TIME-LIFE BOOKS

TIME-LIFE BOOKS, ALEXANDRIA, VIRGINIA

Time-Life Books Inc.
is a wholly owned subsidiary of
TIME INCORPORATED

FOUNDER: Henry R. Luce 1898-1967

Editor-in-Chief: Hedley Donovan
Chairman of the Board: Andrew Heiskell
President: James R. Shepley
Vice Chairman: Roy E. Larsen
Corporate Editors: Ralph Graves, Henry Anatole Grunwald

TIME-LIFE BOOKS INC.
MANAGING EDITOR: Jerry Korn
Executive Editor: David Maness
Assistant Managing Editors: Dale M. Brown, Martin Mann,
John Paul Porter
Art Director: Tom Suzuki
Chief of Research: David L. Harrison
Director of Photography: Robert G. Mason
Planning Director: Thomas Flaherty (acting)
Senior Text Editor: Diana Hirsh
Assistant Art Director: Arnold C. Holeywell
Assistant Chief of Research: Carolyn L. Sackett

CHAIRMAN: Joan D. Manley
President: John D. McSweeney
Executive Vice Presidents: Carl G. Jaeger (U.S. and
Canada), David J. Walsh (International)
Vice President and Secretary: Paul R. Stewart
Treasurer and General Manager: John Steven Maxwell
Business Manager: Peter G. Barnes
Sales Director: John L. Canova
Public Relations Director: Nicholas Benton
Personnel Director: Beatrice T. Dobie
Production Director: Herbert Sorkin
Consumer Affairs Director: Carol Flaumenhaft

THE TIME-LIFE ENCYCLOPEDIA OF GARDENING
EDITORIAL STAFF FOR GARDEN CONSTRUCTION:
EDITOR: Robert M. Jones
Assistant Editor: Sarah Bennett Brash
Text Editors: Bonnie Bohling Kreitler, Bob Menaker
Picture Editors: Jane Jordan, Neil Kagan
Designer: Albert Sherman
Staff Writers: Susan Bryan, Dalton Delan,
Stuart Gannes, Reiko Uyeshima
Researchers: Marilyn Murphy, Susan F. Schneider
Art Assistant: Edwina C. Smith
Editorial Assistant: Maria Zacharias

EDITORIAL PRODUCTION
Production Editor: Douglas B. Graham
Operations Manager: Gennaro C. Esposito
Assistant Production Editor: Feliciano Madrid
Quality Control: Robert L. Young (director),
James J. Cox (assistant), Michael G. Wight (associate)
Art Coordinator: Anne B. Landry
Copy Staff: Susan B. Galloway (chief), Tonna Gibert,
Elizabeth Graham, Florence Keith, Celia Beattie
Picture Department: Dolores A. Littles, Barbara S. Simon

CORRESPONDENTS: Elisabeth Kraemer (Bonn);
Margot Hapgood, Dorothy Bacon (London); Susan Jonas,
Lucy T. Voulgaris (New York); Maria Vincenza Aloisi,
Josephine du Brusle (Paris); Ann Natanson (Rome).
Valuable assistance was also provided by Jacqueline
Schmeal (Houston); Diane Asselin (Los Angeles); Carolyn
T. Chubet, Miriam Hsia (New York). The editors are
indebted to James R. Madison, Rona Mendelsohn, Jane
Opper, Maggie Oster, Susan Perry, Curtis Prendergast, Lee
Lorick Prina and Lyn Stallworth, writers, for their help
with this book.

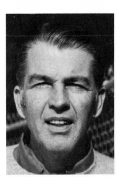

THE AUTHOR: Ogden Tanner, a former staff member of The TIME-LIFE Encyclopedia of Gardening, also wrote *Herbs* for this series and has written or edited volumes on natural history, science and photography. An architectural graduate of Princeton University, he has been associate editor of *House and Home* and assistant managing editor of *Architectural Forum.* Mr. Tanner designed and built many of the structures illustrated in this book.

THE CONSULTANTS: Author of 13 of the volumes in the Encyclopedia, co-author of two additional volumes and consultant on other books in the series, James Underwood Crockett has been a lover of the earth and its good things since his boyhood on a Massachusetts fruit farm. He was graduated from the Stockbridge School of Agriculture at the University of Massachusetts and has worked ever since in horticulture. A perennial contributor to leading gardening magazines, he also writes a monthly bulletin, "Flowery Talks," that is widely distributed through retail florists. His television program, *Crockett's Victory Garden,* shown all over the United States, has won new converts to the Crockett approach to growing things. Lelland L. Gallup is Assistant Professor of Housing and Design at New York State College of Human Ecology, Cornell University, Ithaca, New York. Dr. David S. Ross is an extension agricultural engineer at the University of Maryland, College Park.

THE COVER: A redwood deck, built on two levels to accommodate the slope of this garden, surrounds the four-branched trunk of a magnificent centuries-old California live oak. In the foreground, highlighted by colorful *Cleyera japonica,* railroad ties serve as steps for a path of crushed stone that leads to the deck.

CONTENTS

درختهای انار هم هست کرد اکرد حوض تمام سه برکه زار

The basics of a well-built garden 1

The oldest known garden construction plan, intended for the estate of a wealthy Egyptian who lived approximately 3,300 years ago, depicts trellis-lined walks, garden pools and plant beds. History does not record whether the garden was ever actually constructed, but it had much in common with one that was—the great garden that was built in the 17th Century at Versailles, with its tree-lined walks and shimmering fountains.

Through the ages, every great garden, from the storied Hanging Gardens of Babylon to the Butchart Gardens near Victoria, British Columbia, has consisted of more than a collection of plants. Each was integrated with structural elements that not only made the growing of plants more practical but added beauty in their own right. The next time you go for a walk, take a close look at the most successful gardens in your neighborhood. Near or below nearly every outstanding display of plants you will see some sort of structure that enhances it: a neatly raised plant bed to show off prized perennials, a trellis that displays vines and climbing roses, a reflecting pool that magnifies the garden and provides a cool, refreshing touch on hot summer days.

These structures make any garden more pleasant to work in and to savor, and many are within the capabilities of anyone who can stretch a string between two stakes, hammer a nail through two boards or set bricks on a bed of sand.

One Baltimore gardener had long admired the lovely serpentine brick walls that Thomas Jefferson designed for the University of Virginia campus in Charlottesville and for his beloved estate, Monticello. Although the design seems complex enough to challenge an engineer, during several weekends of leisurely work she built a low version of such a wall beside the terrace in her own backyard. "It was my first experience with bricks and ready-mixed mortar," she told friends who came to admire her handiwork, "but it won't be my

Mongol emperor Babur, who introduced garden construction to India, oversees the building of his Garden of Fidelity at Kabul in 1508. The Persian inscription describes the pomegranate trees surrounding the pool.

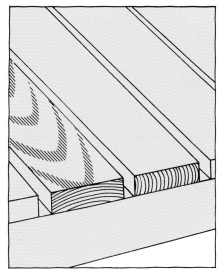

When a log is cut into lumber, its growth rings form patterns visible at the end of each board. If these rings, the wood's grain, parallel the thin edge of a board, the wood is called vertical-grained or quartersawed; if they parallel the faces the wood is called flat-grained or plain-sawed. Either side can face the weather but flat-grained boards should be positioned so the outer convex ring, which was closest to the tree's bark, is exposed. This retards splintering, a bothersome problem on benches, railings and decks.

OUTDOORS, A GRANDER SCALE

last. It was as satisfying as anything I've ever done in the garden—and the wall makes a great background for my begonias."

Of course, she did not just haphazardly slap down some bricks. She took time to study the kind and amount of materials required for her project, including its shallow foundation, and she drew detailed plans in advance, showing how the wall would be built and how it would fit into the overall scheme of her garden. She knew that the curves would give her wall great stability—enough so she did not need any reinforcing rods—but only if she made the depth of the curves at least half the height of the wall. Such planning is the key to success in building any kind of garden structure, from a simple path to an elaborate arbor.

Without an integrated design, the various elements in a series of projects tend to look unrelated, leaving the impression of a busy living room filled with odds and ends accumulated over many years.

Begin your planning by measuring your garden and mapping it to scale. You can make an accurate map with graph paper, letting each square represent one square foot. Be sure to indicate the lay of the land on your map, since hills and hollows will, to a large extent, determine how much of the work you will be able to do yourself. If you are going to want a masonry wall on a slope that is steeper than 30 per cent, for example, special bracing techniques will be required, and you should anticipate leaving that job in the hands of a professional contractor.

Start with the most urgent projects. If your yard is open to passersby, for example, a privacy screen should get top priority. If wind is the most serious problem, plot a fence to break its force before you proceed to more decorative projects. If insects are abundant, find a place to install a bath to attract more birds. In a small city garden with soil that is compacted or exhausted, your first—and perhaps most practical—course may be simply to cover the area over with decorative stones and do your planting in raised beds filled with a fertile potting mix.

As you decide what structures you want and where they should be placed, use stakes and string or lengths of garden hose to mark tentative locations for terraces, paths, walls and other elements. Once you are satisfied that each structure is in the right position and fits well into the overall plan, measure the locations accurately and add them to your scale drawing.

Think large instead of small. A common mistake is to size structures in a garden as though they were inside a house. The outdoors demands a larger scale: elements in your garden will be measured against the outer limits of the property in all directions, including adjacent streets, boundary fences or hedges, high tree branches, even clouds and sky.

Furthermore, outdoor activities, informal and frequently energetic, need plenty of room. If you think, for instance, that a 12-by-12-foot area is about right for a terrace, you probably will enjoy it more if you increase your estimate at the outset and, if you can, make it 14-by-14 or 16-by-16. You can be sure the terrace will be filled all too quickly with furniture, people and plants.

Wherever possible, major walkways should be at least 5 feet wide so two people can walk comfortably abreast rather than Indian file. Garden steps should be generously wide and less steep than indoor stairs. An all-purpose garden bench is typically 6 feet long and 18 inches wide, offering room enough for two people to sit and talk without being crowded or for one person to spread out a few cushions for a sun bath.

Whatever structures you decide to build, keep the design as simple as possible. In a garden, the best-designed elements serve as muted backdrops for plants and people. And the simpler you make something the less it is likely to cost. A loose-stone terrace of crushed rock or gravel, for instance, can be quite adequate, and you can always cover it later, if you wish, with concrete, tile, stone or brick. Similarly, a simple fence made of boards may provide all the privacy you need at a fraction of the cost and time that would be involved in having a stone wall built.

UNOBTRUSIVE BACKGROUNDS

Before you make final plans, check local zoning and building codes to see if they contain any restrictions that apply to your project. The oldest known codes go back to the ancient Babylonian King Hammurabi, whose laws decreed death for any builder whose house collapsed if someone died in the mishap. Today's penalties are hardly that harsh, but modern building codes may be just as stringent about certain things you can and cannot do. You should also check your house deed or neighborhood zoning regulations for special restrictions regarding the setback of structures from property lines, the permissible height of walls and fences, perhaps even the materials you may use to build them.

OFFICIAL GUIDANCE

In most communities, you also will need a building permit for any major permanent structure. Your town or county building inspector will tell you what you can legally build and advise you on how to submit plans. Furthermore, his knowledge of building conditions in your community—the composition of the soil, for example, or the depth of winter frost—can be invaluable.

If you plan a fence or wall near or on a common property line, talk it over with your neighbor. Make sure the fence will be as attractive on his side as it is on yours. You will avoid ill will if you do so, and you may even get him to share the cost.

Before undertaking major work, you may want to consult with professional landscape architects. They have the training, and usually the imagination and taste, to prepare a comprehensive program that you can execute over a period of years if you like. Most landscape architects are willing to confer on an hourly fee basis before making general recommendations.

USING PROFESSIONAL HELP

Once your plans are firm, decide what work you can handle and what should be done by a contractor. Major grading and drainage projects—driveways and large retaining walls, for example—are best left in the hands of professionals who have the necessary heavy equipment. On some jobs, though, you can have a contractor do the heavy part of the work, then do the lighter but more time-consuming part yourself. For instance, you could hire a concrete specialist to dig holes and pour footings for a sizable deck, then complete above-ground work at your convenience.

If you have had little building experience, try small projects first. You can build a wooden plant container, a window box or a birdhouse *(page 16)* indoors on winter evenings or rainy Sundays, using these projects to develop your skills for larger outdoor jobs that you can tackle when the weather is right.

SIX WAYS TO JOIN BOARDS

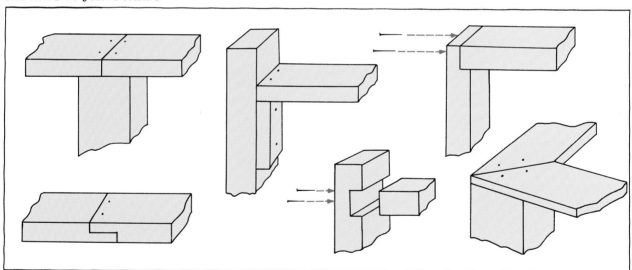

Two boards, butted end-to-end and nailed to a supporting upright (top), form a basic, utilitarian joint. Matching notches cut in two boards and glued and nailed together (bottom) form a stronger joint that sheds water.

Glue and nail a block to the face of an upright to support a horizontal piece (top). For a stronger joint, saw and chisel a notch into the upright (bottom) and glue and nail the end of the horizontal board into it.

To join two boards at right angles, notch one to the thickness of the other; glue and nail them together (top). For a miter joint atop an upright, saw the two horizontal pieces at 45° angles and nail in place (bottom).

Whether you handle a garden construction project yourself or hire someone to build it, you need to be familiar with the advantages and limitations of materials that might be used. Choose materials that are appropriate for the job, that will blend comfortably with your house and garden, that will stand up under local weather for many years, that are available at a reasonable cost and that are not difficult to work with.

The encyclopedia of construction materials on pages 140-153 will help you choose those materials that are best for your project. But compare available materials and costs by visiting a number of suppliers: lumber and building-supply companies, nurseries and garden centers, masonry-product yards, even wrecking company salvage yards where you may find bargains in used materials. One Cleveland handyman, with the help of a few friends armed with crowbars, was able to salvage a large old storage shed near his home. The wood had weathered beautifully to a silvery-gray patina; it was well worth hours of pulling old nails to make the old lumber usable. The fence that the gardener and his friends built from the old boards blended serenely into the background and looked as though it had enclosed his garden for generations.

Most building materials are cheaper if you haul them home yourself. If you are buying large amounts of lumber or a heavy material like flagstone, balance the cost of delivery against that of renting a truck or trailer for the day. If you do have the materials delivered, have them unloaded as close as possible to your work site. Flagstones, concrete blocks, bricks and other heavy materials should be stacked neatly to prevent breakage.

When you choose materials, consider what you and your helpers can reasonably accomplish without undue strain. A brick weighs about 4 pounds, but a concrete block weighs about 40 or 50 pounds, a 1-cubic-foot sack of cement weighs 94 pounds, and a sizable flagstone (thick enough to be used in a terrace laid on sand) can weigh more than 100 pounds—enough to give someone unaccustomed to handling them a serious injury. When you lift a heavy object, keep your back as straight as possible, flexing your knees and using the large leg muscles to take the brunt of the load. For moving loads of materials, a well-balanced utility cart with two rubber-tired wheels is easier to handle, has greater capacity and is less likely to tip than an ordinary wheelbarrow.

HEAVY LOADS TO LIFT

Of all garden building materials, wood is the most widely used. It is suitable for everything from edging strips to decks. It is very much at home among growing plants, and is relatively light in weight and easy to handle. Wood is classified as either hardwood or soft-

11

wood. Hardwoods such as oak, maple and walnut are generally used indoors; they are too expensive for most garden construction. The mainstays of garden construction are softwoods such as hemlock, fir, spruce, pine, redwood, cedar and cypress. These softwoods, from cone-bearing, needle-leaved trees, are easier to cut as well as less expensive than hardwoods.

HOW WOOD IS GRADED

Softwoods are graded by quality. The designations of quality may vary depending on where you live in the United States or Canada *(page 153)*. Boards marked Select A or B, or B and Better, or First and Second Quality, or No. 1 and 2 Clear are nearly flawless—and too good for anything but fine cabinet work. Even lumber that is marked Select C and D, with small imperfections, is better than a garden builder needs. Most garden projects can be built with lumber that is graded No. 1 Common through No. 4 Common. No. 5 Common, which may have large holes, splits and other defects, has some limited uses, such as in subflooring and for temporary bracing.

Load-bearing structural lumber is graded by strength. It is best to use Construction or Standard grades for framing. Use Utility and Economy grades only for temporary bracing or concrete forms.

Redwood is naturally insect- and rot-resistant; it is widely used for outdoor decks, benches, fences and siding. It has a special grading system *(page 153)* based not only on imperfections but also on the amount of heartwood a piece of lumber contains. The heartwood, from the center of a tree, is a rich red or cinammon color, in contrast to the yellow or cream-colored sapwood from the outer trunk. Heartwood contains more of the natural chemicals that resist decay. The top grades of redwood are too luxurious for most garden uses; garden grades are Construction Heart and Construction Common. The most economical grade, Merchantable, can be used judiciously for rustic fencing and other rough construction.

WEEDING OUT THE DEFECTS

When you buy lumber, inspect each piece. Avoid boards with especially large or loose knots, splits and rough or damaged edges. Lay long boards on the floor or some other flat surface to check against warping. If you should find a warped board in your order, you may be able to straighten it by wetting the board, placing it on a pair of supports and weighting it in the middle for several days *(opposite page)*. You can also glue loose knots in place. But, within the limitations of the grade of lumber you are buying, it is better to avoid major imperfections in the first place.

Boards are sold in 2-foot increments, from 8 to 20 feet long. The thickness and width of a board are given in the dimensions it had when it was rough-cut from the tree; these dimensions are referred to as "nominal" sizes. However, except for lumber that has been left rough for rustic applications, the wood you purchase will have been smoothed on all sides and stamped "S4S" for "surfaced four sides." In the surfacing process, the measurements of the board are reduced by the amount of rough wood removed; the piece also shrinks as it dries. Thus, the common 2-by-4 actually measures 1½ by 3½ inches. For a table comparing nominal and actual lumber sizes, see page 151.

Most retail yards sell lumber by the linear foot, but the basis for pricing is the board foot, a unit 1 foot long, 1 nominal foot wide and 1 nominal inch thick. To find the number of board feet in a piece of wood, multiply its nominal thickness in inches by its nominal width in inches by its actual length in feet, then divide by 12. A 2-by-10 that is 6 feet long, for example, contains 2 times 10 times 6, or 120 divided by 12, or 10 board feet. If you buy a lot of lumber the yard may give you a quote "per thousand," which will be a slightly lower price based on the cost of 1,000 board feet.

In addition to boards—lumber with a nominal thickness less than 2 inches—wood comes in larger pieces, called dimensional lumber (2 to 5 inches thick) and timbers (5 or more inches in width and thickness). It also comes in smaller pieces called strips, including laths, battens and grape stakes. These latter pieces are useful for light fencing, trellises and arbors, where narrow, spaced members are desired for an airy effect.

One of the most popular of building materials is plywood, those panels made from thin plies of wood that are glued together with the

FROM LATHS TO TIMBERS

STRAIGHTENING A WARPED BOARD

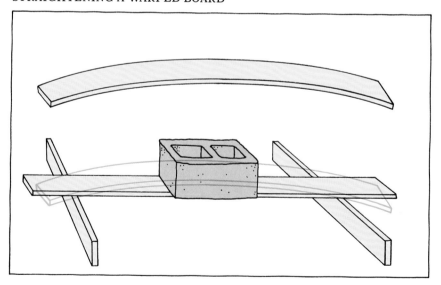

If you have a board that is bowed but not cupped or twisted (top), you can reduce the warp enough to make it usable in a fence or deck. First dampen the warp with water to make it more flexible. Prop the ends of the board, with the warped side up, on wood scraps or bricks and center a cinder block or other heavy weight on the bow (bottom). Keep the underside damp; in a few days the warp will relax enough so the board can be used in your project.

grains running in alternate directions to give strength and stability. Most common plywoods are made from softwoods like fir, spruce, lauan or pine; they are graded by the quality of the outer plies. A panel stamped "A-C," for example, is top quality on the front, a lower quality, with knots and patches, on the back (table, page 153). Interior plywood should be used only indoors; exterior plywoods are required for garden construction because their plies have been joined with waterproof glue so the panels can stand up to the weather once they are treated to protect the wood. Exterior plywood comes in standard 4-by-8-foot panels that range from one quarter to three quarters of an inch in thickness. For a garden shelter or fence where a decorative appearance is desirable, plywood is available prefinished in a grooved pattern that resembles planking.

NATURAL ROT RESISTANCE   In almost all garden construction, some pieces of wood will be exposed to moisture, alternate freezing and thawing, and attack by insects and the organisms that cause rot. The kind of wood you choose for your projects should depend on the severity of these conditions. Many professionals prefer to use redwood because of its natural rot-resistance; cedar and cypress are popular for the same reason. These woods can be left unfinished and in time will weather to a silvery gray, or they can be finished with a pigmented stain that will enhance the natural color and grain. The use of a clear water repellent intended for outdoor use will give adequate protection against discoloration without changing the color of the wood. But varnish and similar clear film finishes are generally unsuitable for outdoor use; varnish in particular may turn yellow and crack if it is exposed to moisture and sun.

CHOOSING A PRESERVATIVE   Less rot-resistant—but also less expensive—are such softwoods as fir, spruce and pine. They can be used in a garden if they are protected with a wood preservative. Creosote, the oldest preservative on the market, is effective but messy to work with, leaving a black, oily, unpaintable residue that is toxic to plants and animals. So creosote should be used only below ground and several feet away from plants. Many newer preservatives contain pentachlorophenol; they leave a light, paintable residue, but they may also poison plants. Wood that is treated with pentachlorophenol should be allowed to dry at least a week before being used near plants. The safest wood preservatives to use in the garden are products with a copper base, such as copper naphthenate or copper sulfate. They can be bought in clear form or as colored stains, or they can be covered with stain or paint after drying.

Any preservative must penetrate well into the wood to ensure its effectiveness. Fence posts, plant-bed edgings and other wood that will be in contact with the soil or exposed to severe weather should be placed directly in the preservative *(below)*. After such pieces have been cut to size, stand them in large cans of preservative long enough to protect the vulnerable end grain. Even more effective protection is available in lumber that has been pressure-treated with a preservative at a factory. Such wood can be bought as boards, structural members, plywood and timbers called landscape ties. Similar to railroad ties, landscape ties can be used to build steps, retaining walls and raised plant beds. Clean, nontoxic and odor-free, pressure-treated wood can be used in the garden with no additional preservative. Its pale greenish hue will eventually weather to gray, or it can be painted or stained. Test stakes of pressure-treated wood have shown no significant deterioration after more than a quarter of a century in the ground.

Your handiwork will be spoiled, no matter what kind of wood you use, if you choose hardware that leaves streaks of rust. If appearance is important, use nails, bolts and hinges made of an aluminum alloy, brass or stainless steel. For less demanding projects, galvanized fasteners are adequate.

As a general rule, a nail should be three times as long as the thickness of the wood it holds, so that two thirds of the nail penetrates the backup piece. When a nail that long is impractical,

RUSTPROOF HARDWARE

A PENETRATING SOAK TO WARD OFF ROT

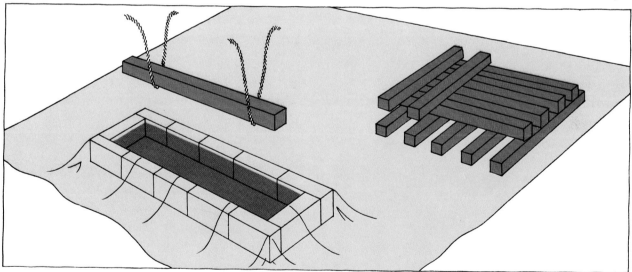

A soaking trough, built on bare ground with cinder-block walls and lined with several sheets of polyethylene plastic, makes a temporary vat for treating lumber with wood preservative. Additional large sheets of plastic nearby will provide a place to stack treated boards. Wearing rubber gloves, fill the trough with a copper-based wood preservative that is not toxic to plants. Use ropes as slings to lower boards into the liquid. Leave the boards submerged for a day, then lift them out, stack them in alternating rows (right) and let them dry for at least two days. Save leftover preservative for reuse.

one that is driven 1½ inches into supporting wood will usually hold. If a nail penetrates the backup piece, bend the point over flush with the wood; the resulting connection will be very strong, even if it does not look very professional. Neater solutions are to use a shorter nail driven in at an angle for greater holding power or to use the kind of nails with rings or threads around their shanks or with a rosin coating designed to give them a strong grip. Nails that are driven parallel with the wood grain, that is, into the end of a piece of lumber, have little holding power; if you cannot avoid such joints use the longest possible nails.

HOW TO PREVENT SPLITS

A row of nails driven in a straight line may split a board. To avoid this, stagger the nails so that they do not line up along the grain. You can also forestall splitting by blunting the points of the nails, giving each a tap or two with a hammer. The blunt point shears the wood fibers instead of wedging them apart. An even more effective method is to drill pilot holes of a slightly smaller diameter than that of the nails.

For joints that must bear heavy loads, such as those in supporting railings and decks, use fasteners with more holding power than nails—galvanized wood screws for smaller pieces, lag screws or bolts for larger ones. Plant containers that will hold heavy loads of wet soil may require joints that are glued before they are screwed together.

A SNUG HOUSE FOR BLUEBIRDS

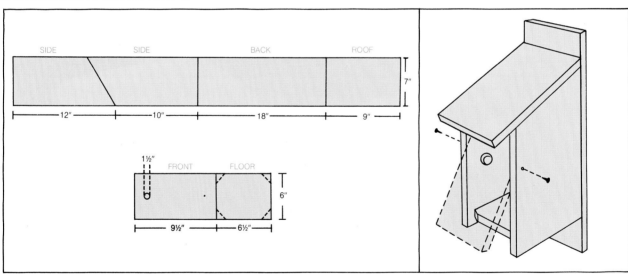

The panels for a bluebird house can be cut from ¾-inch exterior-grade plywood or from weather-resistant redwood. Cut the tops of the side walls at an angle of about 60° so the roof will shed water. For ventilation, make

the front panel ½ inch shorter than the sides, and trim off the corners of the bottom piece to allow drainage. Drill two screw-mounting holes in the back panel, and use a 1½-inch bit to cut the bluebird entry hole.

Assemble the birdhouse panels with eightpenny coated nails. Attach the front with nail pivots through the sides; secure it to the floor with an eye screw. Mount the house 8 feet from the ground, facing away from the wind.

For this, use a waterproof adhesive such as epoxy resin, acrylic or resorcinol resin.

Most garden projects can be built with only the tools most homeowners already have. If you need certain specialized tools, you usually can save money by renting them for a few days. But whether you are using a rented concrete mixer or a claw hammer to pull out a nail, the following common-sense rules will make your work easier and safer:

● Do not stuff pointed tools or sharp nails into a pocket. Carry them in a tool belt or in a carpenter's apron.

● Check metal-headed tools such as hammers and files to be sure the heads are firmly attached to the handles.

● Keep cutting tools such as saws and chisels sharp and clean. Dull edges slow the work and can slip easily because extra pressure has to be applied to them.

● Do not wear loose sleeves, shirttails, neckties or jewelry when you are working with tools. They get in the way, and they can be caught in power tools. If you have long hair, tie it back out of the way or tuck it under a hat.

● When you use any power tool, be sure the cord is kept well away from the cutting blade or drill bit. Many craftsmen drape the cord over their shoulders so they have no doubt where it is. Do not carry a power tool by its cord; be sure to disconnect the tool from its power source when you change bits or blades.

● Do not use a power tool where the earth or other surface is wet or where the light is poor.

● Do not force a power tool. It will perform better and more safely at the speed and pressure for which it was designed.

● Always wear wrap-around plastic safety glasses or goggles when you are using a power saw and when you are drilling, hammering or cutting masonry.

● Finally, do not hesitate to use special equipment or clothing to make the job safer and more comfortable: heavy work gloves to protect your hands when you are using rough materials; earplugs or clamp-on ear protectors if you are working with a noisy machine; a respirator or filter mask if you are spray painting or using a power tool that produces a lot of dust.

It is also a good idea to wear strap-on rubber kneepads when you lay brick or trowel concrete. After all, building your own terrace, path or planting bed is going to be more work than recreation if you wind up with sore knees, cut fingers or an aching back. In garden construction, as in gardening, it is possible to enjoy the work as well as the results.

Grand illusions in small spaces

Urban dwellers faced with the emptiness of a tiny walled garden often must exercise more ingenuity than their country cousins. City gardens are plagued with problems—not only cramped space for plantings, and walls that cast dark shadows, but often soil too poor to nourish the scraggiest patch of grass.

The most successful city gardeners have discovered that such disadvantages can be overcome with garden construction that is practical as well as decorative. Some of the most eye-pleasing garden embellishments open up new horticultural possibilities as well. Raised beds can be filled with soil ready-mixed to suit the most exacting exotics. Several planters, using a variety of soil types, make it possible to raise widely different species within a few feet of each other. The drabbest wall, dressed up with a trellis, will run rampant with shade-tolerant vines.

By virtue of their design, these same constructions will also round out corners and break up the stark wall surfaces that give small gardens a claustrophobic, boxy feeling. To make them fit comfortably in pocket-sized plots, new structures should be kept in scale with the garden's proportions; building materials should complement the plants they hold and harmonize with existing structures.

The greatest attraction in tackling garden-construction projects may be the fact that amateurs can often achieve stunning results on the first try. Anyone timid about putting trowel to mortar should be encouraged by the story of the lady who set out without prior experience to lay a garden floor of brick. She had three cubic yards of sand, weighing nearly four tons, dumped into her walled garden, then went after it with a rake and shovel until it was as smooth as a wave-washed beach. Meticulously she laid out bricks in two ever-widening concentric circles measured with a string staked at the center of each. When every brick was tamped in place, a friend asked permission to copy the masterpiece and sent a terrace designer to have a look. The pro was so impressed he not only had a look; he asked the amateur for a tutoring session on her techniques.

*Raised beds transform a 15-by-17-foot
garden into a luxuriant outdoor dining space.
House plants taking the late spring air
(left) hide a storage bin.*

Fashioning a focal point

Creating a focus that will lead the eye away from a walled garden's cramped dimensions calls for careful planning and imaginative construction. Fortunately, the human eye instinctively zeroes in on the most prominent object in a small space. If a gardener subordinates everything to the scale and color of an attention-grabbing centerpiece, the eye will be tricked into seeing the most minute patch of earth as a spacious stretch of land.

A sylvan grotto grown thick with variegated caladiums and ferns fills the corner of a tiny walled garden. From a concealed hose, water trickles down the remains of an old wall through a rubble of rock that provides a sloping bed for the shade-loving plants. Although fast-growing bamboo (right) must be constantly trimmed down to scale, the ivy and periwinkle in the raised beds at the foot of the rocks are virtually care free.

Dainty as a Victorian valentine, this small garden focuses on
a nymph-graced fountain accented by a brick arch. The classical
style is complemented by subdued frills of color scattered
among the stately boxwood and espaliered ivy.

Climbing up the sides of the house on a construction of
chicken wire and lead anchor strips, a wisteria vine not only
frames the porch with a striking mass of greenery but also
provides a backdrop to unify the display of blooming annuals.

21

Avoiding tunnel visions

Even a lot that is as long and lonely as a bowling alley can be given an air of enchanting elegance by the artful application of construction techniques. The trick is to build intriguing curves, interesting contours, even teasing blind spots to fascinate the viewer. In narrow gardens where every subtle variation adds to a sense of fullness, plants can heighten the effect if strategically placed with dark greens against light greens, broad leaves against narrow.

"I have never believed in square corners; curving lines are more inviting," says the owner of this 15-by-100-foot garden who has camouflaged its narrow dimensions with deeply undulating, brick-edged beds. Off-center urns of bright geraniums and a birdbath cannily set in a rear corner divert the eye from a straight-down-the-center view.

The circular pattern of bricks paving this garden not only relieves the monotony of the angular walls but visually seems to widen the 15-by-50-foot space where cryptomeria (right) and dogwood (left, rear) grow out of narrow, serpentine beds. The brick paving slopes slightly to drain toward the back.

Plant pockets at center stage

Depending on its uses, the best allocation of space in a tiny lot is often a garden within a garden. To sacrifice the central and often the sunniest spot to an empty expanse of paving seems a prodigal waste to many small-yard gardeners who covet every inch for planting beds. By placing a garden pocket center stage, design-savvy gardeners can also come up with a scene-stealing showpiece if they enhance the area with visually interesting construction.

Front and center, a phalanx of tulips in a diamond-shaped bed commands attention in a garden that has been divided to meet a family's needs. The geometric beds satisfy the gardener and leave room for other family members to swing in a hammock (left) or play in the sand (right, rear). The dwarf Kingsville boxwoods edging the beds need no clipping.

Rounded English boxwood, ruffly miniature roses and peonies soften the austere formality of this 20-by-20-foot garden fashioned from a square within a square. A winsome statue, raised to eye level atop a brick-enclosed birdbath swathed in ivy, casts a reflective air over the angular brick walks.

Ivy-covered brick edging that tops off a natural clay slope imitates the look of a rural retaining wall in this 27-by-90-foot garden. Instead of grading the slope, the owner turned it into an asset by using it to divide the garden into two levels. Steps built a bit crookedly and off-center plus a meandering flagstone walk enlarge upon the rustic theme.

Floors for a great outdoors 2

As more and more people discover the pleasures of outdoor living, one of their top priorities often becomes the construction of some kind of deck, patio or terrace where they can observe how the garden grows, read the Sunday paper, eat a pleasant meal, enjoy a sun bath or entertain friends. For some, such an outdoor living room may include a children's play area, a sheltered work space for potting plants or a comfortable garden path that invites an intimate look at the flowers. For most of these garden activities you will want an artificial surface that is attractive, durable, easy to maintain and safe to use in all kinds of weather.

Purists may avow that a garden is not a garden without a lot of grass, but getting grass to grow can be a losing battle. When a lawn is subjected to heavy traffic near the house, especially in a damp and shady spot, it can quickly become a muddy disaster area. Sooner or later even the most ardent grassgrower concedes this fact, and though he may keep the rest of his yard planted with grass, he generally chooses a less perishable kind of carpeting to cover the outdoor living areas.

Such outdoor flooring ranges from loose, soft materials that can be simply spread on the ground to permanent installations of wood planking, bricks or concrete. Among the least expensive are such organic products as wood chips, sawdust, bark chunks and shredded bark. One enterprising gardener who lives near a flour mill in upstate New York has an intricate network of paths surfaced with buckwheat hulls. "When the hulls pack down or blow away," he says, "I just go back to the mill for more."

Such materials are more than adequate for simple, rustic paths where the main objective is to avoid trudging through mud. They also make good mulches to spread around plants to conserve moisture and add protection from weather. Shredded bark, tanbark in particular, provides a springy, clean surface for play yards, where it

Stone steps bordered with boulders help complete a garden designed by Thomas Church, father of modern American garden construction. The pebble aggregate at bottom gives way to redwood chips at the top.

can be piled under slides and swings to cushion inevitable falls.

To keep loose material from being scattered, many gardeners dig out several inches of sod or topsoil, add gravel for drainage and line the edges with bricks or rot-resistant boards set on edge to confine the top layer of bark or wood chips.

LOOSE-STONE WALKWAYS

For a somewhat dressier, more durable surface, some landscapers prefer such inorganic materials as pulverized rock, gravel or crushed stone. Those that are finely pulverized—red rock, decomposed granite, dolomite or crushed brick—are applied in two 3-inch layers, each moistened and then compacted with a heavy garden roller. Despite this treatment, these finely pulverized materials may become dusty. Larger chunks of crushed rock or gravel are cleaner and more likely to stay in place. They can be spread over a layer of pulverized material or directly on the ground. Like other loose materials, these need to be contained by wood edgings or by bricks laid to form a mowing strip. (A mowing strip is a hard, flat surface flush with the ground adjoining the edge of a lawn; one wheel of the lawn mower runs along this strip, eliminating the need for most tedious hand trimming.)

Gravel consists of rounded pebbles ranging from ¼ inch in diameter to an inch or more, and comes in shades of white, tan and black. Some decorative gravels are available in hues of gray-blue, maroon and even gold. The smallest size, pea gravel, has a formal look but must be raked to keep it looking neat. The ½-inch size is more practical; heels and furniture legs are less likely to sink into it and it is heavy enough to stay in place. Larger stones are not as comfortable to walk on, but they provide an additional bold touch in the design and they make convenient and care-free drainage beds for displays of potted plants.

COMPACTED FOR STABILITY

Crushed rock, man-made from larger rocks and often called quarry stone, is the most stable of loose-stone surfacing materials because its sharp, angular facets interlock tightly. When compacted with a heavy roller it can be used for driveways and service yards as well as for terraces and paths. For a durable 4- to 6-inch bed of crushed rock, a 2- to 3-inch layer of stones up to 2 inches in diameter is placed and compacted, then is topped with a layer of smaller, ½-inch stones. For a smoother surface, a topping of rock dust is brushed into the crevices to bind the stones before they are moistened and rolled for the final time.

Weeds are bound to pop up through any loose paving material. Covering the soil beneath with roofing felt or heavy black sheet plastic will cut down on the number of weeds that will surface. Punch holes in the sheeting every foot or so in all directions to let water and air penetrate to any underlying tree roots and to allow the surface to dry quickly after a rain.

Most loose stone is sold by the cubic yard. To avoid the possibility of your garden looking like a prison rock pile because you ordered too much material, use the following formula when you order: multiply the length of the area to be surfaced by its width in feet, and by the desired depth of stone in fractions of a foot, then divide that number by 27, the number of cubic feet in a cubic yard. Thus, a 20-by-20-foot terrace to be covered with 4 inches of gravel will require 20 times 20 times ⅓, divided by 27, or 4.9 cubic yards, rounded off to 5 cubic yards to allow for some spillage and waste.

Gravel is an attractive choice for any homeowner on a tight budget. But many people who could afford any material prefer gravel's natural appearance and the soft, rustling crunch it makes underfoot. If you like, you can combine gravel with more solid paving materials.

BUDGET-WISE GRAVEL

A certain small terrace behind a New York brownstone house is one of the most popular stops on neighborhood garden tours because the owner has combined paving materials with plants in a very imaginative way. The terrace is divided into sections with redwood 2-by-4s set on edge and nailed together. The sections of the terrace that are used for entertaining are paved with reclaimed brick, while

CUTTING BRICKS AND FLAGSTONES

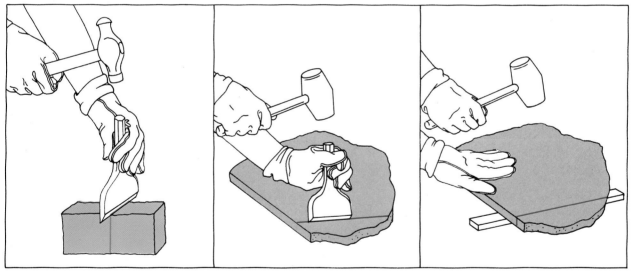

Cut paving bricks cleanly with a mason's brickset. Wearing goggles and gloves, score the brick by tapping the brickset with a hammer. Then, with the brickset bevel facing away from the part to be used, strike a sharp blow.

The first step in trimming a flagstone or other rock is to cushion it in sand. Then, wearing gloves and goggles, score a line on the rock by rapping a brickset or a stonemason's chisel with a steel-headed mallet.

The second step in trimming flagstone: prop the scored stone on a scrap of wood, letting the unwanted segment overhang the edge. Tap this piece with the mallet until it breaks off. If necessary, score the bottom as well.

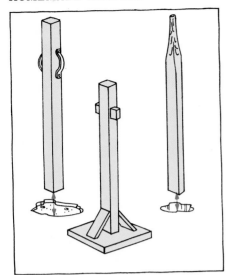

*A homemade tamper, fashioned
from scrap lumber, is useful for packing
down the fill that will underlay
concrete or pavers. To compact coarse
stone or rubble, fasten screen-door
handles to opposite sides of a chest-high
length of 4-by-4 (left). For leveling
and firming soil or sand, attach handles
and a braced square of plywood to a
4-by-4 (center). A 2-by-4 that is 4 or 5
feet long and has a rounded top for
gripping makes a good tool for tamping
the fill around fence posts (right).*

BRICKS MADE TO WALK ON

other sections outside the normal traffic flow are filled with gravel and sculptural rocks. The hardy cacti scattered among the rocks draw a lot of comment, but the mixed-media terrace is a conversation piece in itself.

The palette of materials available for hard-paving a portion of your garden ranges from bricks and concrete blocks of many kinds to stone slabs and poured concrete. Wood, glareproof and comfortable to walk on, is generally the material of choice for elevated decks on sloping sites, but it too can be used to make terrace paving blocks or low platforms on level ground.

Of all the materials used for garden paving, brick probably is the most popular with weekend handymen. It is available in some 10,000 combinations of sizes, shapes, colors and textures and is equally at home in a casual or a formal setting. Bricks are of a size and weight easily handled by anyone and thus are especially suitable for family projects. A homeowner who lays bricks on a bed of sand does not have to hurry frantically in a race with hardening mortar; he can put down as many as he feels up to in one session, take a break and return to the project later. If more than a few hours will elapse, however, cover the edge bricks with a board to make sure they do not shift. Despite this casual approach, a properly chosen and installed loose-brick floor will last for many years. It has the additional advantage of being skid resistant and it will not glare or become excessively hot to the touch.

There are three basic kinds of bricks: common, face and paving. Common bricks, also called building bricks, are the most widely available and least costly. Most come in a reddish shade and measure 7½ to 8 inches long, 3¼ to 3½ inches wide and 2¼ inches thick. Some common bricks are made with holes for lightness and stronger mortar bonding. They are suitable for paving only if they are set on edge; this requires half again as many bricks as needed for flat paving. Other common bricks are so soft and porous they crumble under repeated freezing. These should be used outdoors only in dry, mild climates.

Face bricks, often used in the walls of commercial buildings, come in many sizes and colors and in textures ranging from shaggy rough to glassy smooth. Face bricks are not always available through retail outlets but if you can locate them, you will have an excellent paving material.

The best choice of all for outdoor flooring is paving bricks— which is not surprising since they are made specifically for that purpose. Paving bricks are available in some 40 different shapes and sizes and in a wide variety of textures and colors, from red to off-white, yellow, chocolate brown and even pink. Paving bricks are made in the usual brick dimensions and also come as thin as half an inch. The thinner types are laid like tiles in a bed of concrete. You can buy rectangular paving bricks as wide as 4 inches and as long as 11¾ inches, in square shapes from 4 to 16 inches on a side and in hexagons 6, 12 and 18 inches across. Unlike common and face bricks, which are proportioned to allow space for mortar joints, the length of some rectangular paving bricks is exactly twice their width, so they can be laid tightly without using any mortar and still come out evenly in any pattern.

Some brick patterns, such as jack-on-jack (aligned joints) and basket weave (widths and lengths alternating) can be laid without cutting bricks. Others, such as running bond and herringbone,

PAVING WITH LOOSE BRICKS

1. *To level a bed of coarse sand for a walk of loose bricks, make a screed from a 2-by-4 plank (page 40), cutting the lower part to the width of the walk. Pour 2 inches of sand inside a permanent frame of rot-resistant wood, set into a trench 4½ inches deep, and supported temporarily with 12-inch stakes. Before leveling, soak the sand with a fine spray from a garden hose.*

2. *Roll out lengths of 30-pound asphalt building paper on top of the bed of sand to serve as a weed barrier. When the paper is in place, puncture it with rows of drainage holes at 4- to 6-inch intervals.*

3. *Lay the paving bricks closely together on top of a thin layer of sand spread over the building paper. Tamp each brick into place with a rubber mallet or the wooden handle of a trowel, adding or removing sand as necessary to keep the walk level.*

4. *Use a push broom to sweep fine, dry sand across the walk to fill any gaps that could permit the bricks to shift. Sweep diagonally across the joints to avoid brushing out the top layer of sand. When all the joints are filled, hose down the walk. Fill the trench outside the frame and remove the stakes.*

require cutting where the pattern meets a straight edge. You cut a brick by striking it sharply with a brickmason's hammer or with a hammer and broad-bladed chisel, called a brickset, with the beveled edge facing the piece to be cut off. If you cut bricks (or any other hard material) be certain you wear gloves and don safety goggles to protect your eyes from flying chips.

RATED FOR THE WEATHER

In areas where freezing and thawing cause soft brick to flake or crack, choose bricks for their resistance to local weather as well as resistance to abrasion. The most reliable way of buying bricks is to select them according to grade. A brick rated NW (no weathering) is too soft to be used for paving; a brick with an MW (moderate weathering) can be used in mild, dry regions. A brick with an SW rating (severe weathering) is best if the paving must stand up to extreme weather conditions.

Some retailers have old, used bricks for sale; they may cost more than new bricks but occasionally you can get them free at demolition sites. Such bricks are often very handsome in a garden, and if they come from exterior walls they have already passed the test of time. But after you have spent days sorting out broken pieces and chipping off bits of old mortar, you may decide used bricks are more costly than they seem.

QUICK EDGINGS FOR PLANT BEDS

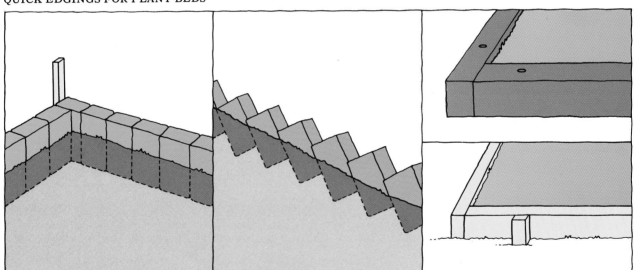

Vertical rows of paving bricks set on end make a simple but attractive curb around a bed of plants. Stake out and dig shallow trenches along the perimeter of the bed, sink the bricks halfway into the ground and pack earth firmly around them.

You can make a saw-tooth edging pattern with paving bricks by tilting each one at a 45° angle. When you pack earth carefully along this brick border you create the illusion of a row of neat brick triangles resting on the surface of the ground.

For wood edgings that will contain raised plant beds, use heavy railroad ties (top) pegged to the ground with 12-inch steel pipes, or preservative-treated 2-by-6s (bottom). Join the 2-by-6s with galvanized spikes and brace them with 12-inch stakes.

When you order bricks, compare types, prices and delivery charges at two or more yards. As a rule of thumb, five standard bricks set tightly without mortar will cover 1 square foot, as will four and one half paver bricks with 4-by-8-inch faces or four and one half standard bricks with ½-inch mortar joints. Add about 5 per cent to the number of bricks you need to allow for breakage and replacement. A 20-by-20-foot terrace may need more than 2,000 standard-sized bricks, but do not be put off by the numbers; brick is less expensive than most other paving materials. To avoid extra handling and breakage, ask that your order be delivered strapped to a wooden pallet, not dumped in a pile.

THE EASIEST HARD SURFACE

If the soil in your yard drains quickly and is not subject to heaving frosts, you can make a path or small terrace of bricks without any prepared base at all. Strip off sod and topsoil to a depth half an inch less than the thickness of the brick, or 1 inch less in soft soil to allow for settling. Level the excavation with the back of a garden rake. If you contain the edges of the area with bricks set on end, the internal bricks will shift very little under moderate traffic and weather conditions.

For a more permanent installation, set the bricks in a bed of sand or on poured concrete. Laying bricks on sand, the most popular

A RECIPE FOR GARDEN CONCRETE

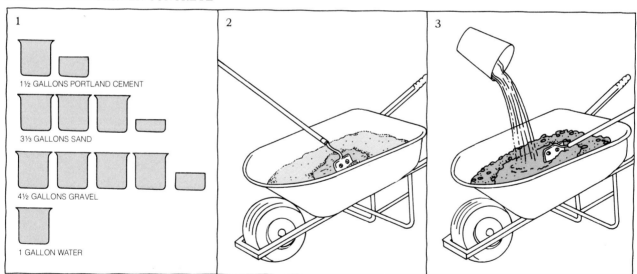

1

1½ GALLONS PORTLAND CEMENT

3⅓ GALLONS SAND

4½ GALLONS GRAVEL

1 GALLON WATER

2

3

The containers above indicate the proper ratio, in gallons, of portland cement, sand, gravel and water necessary to make 1 cubic foot of concrete suitable for garden paving. If you make larger batches, increase the ingredients proportionately.

With a hoe, mix the dry ingredients in a wheelbarrow. Start with a center pile of cement ringed by a doughnut of sand. When this mixture is uniform in color, shape it into another ring, add coarse gravel in the center and mix together again.

Pour about three fourths of the water into a scooped-out cavity in the dry mixture. Hoe the mix into the water gradually until it is all soaked up. Repeat this process as you slowly add the remaining water or until the concrete is workable but not wet.

TERRACE OR PATIO?

Americans call just about any kind of outdoor living area a patio, but the correct name for that slab of concrete outside the recreation-room door is terrace. Though some people associate terraces with the grand style of country manors, the word is a workaday term that architects use for any sort of outdoor paved area, whether it is raised or at ground level, freestanding or attached to the house. Patio, a word borrowed from the Spaniards who settled in California, properly applies only to courtyards enclosed on all sides by house or garden walls. During the building boom that followed World War II, real-estate salesmen in the Southwest fast-talked the corrupted meaning into popularity.

DRY-MORTAR JOINTS

do-it-yourself method, is not difficult. You can easily replace damaged bricks and reset any that are heaved up by frost. Because water drains through the open joints, the surface dries quickly, and the water will penetrate to any tree roots below. Many gardeners prefer this method because they can build a planting pocket wherever they want simply by pulling out a few bricks.

A 2-inch layer of builder's sand is adequate for a loose-brick terrace if drainage is good. But if the soil is soggy or heavy with clay, put down a 3- to 4-inch base of coarse gravel or crushed rock before spreading the bed of sand. To guard against water damage, the finished brick surface should slope away from the foundation of the house; in areas of heavy rainfall or poor drainage, the surface should drop 1 inch in every 4 to 6 feet. Perforated draintile or plastic tubing can be used in the gravel layer to channel water away from especially wet spots.

Before you place bricks, wet the sand bed with a fine spray from a garden hose, then level it by pulling the edge of a board across it. Then, starting at one corner, tap each brick firmly into place with the butt of a garden trowel or the handle of a hammer, checking the surface frequently with a carpenter's level. As you progress, kneel on the completed brick surface so that you will not disturb the sand layer.

When you have placed all the bricks, spread fine sand on top of them. Sweep the sand back and forth until the joints are filled, then brush off any excess, sweeping on a diagonal with the joints so you do not scoop the sand out of them.

If you prefer the look of open joints, or if variations in brick sizes require you to open the joints to make a pattern come out even, dry mortar will stabilize the bricks and discourage weeds. To make dry mortar, mix 1 part portland cement with 6 parts of sand and brush it over the paved surface. Sweep off any excess mixture, then mist the surface of the terrace or walkway with a fine spray from the garden hose to set the mortar. If the misting causes too much settling, repeat the procedure.

Paving bricks larger than ordinary bricks, precast concrete pavers and flagstones can also be laid on soil or in sand. Precast concrete pavers come in a variety of shapes, sizes and colors. Most lumber yards and masonry suppliers sell pavers 2 inches thick with face sizes of 8-by-16 inches, 12-by-12 inches, 16-by-16 inches and 18-by-18 inches. You may also be able to find smaller sizes such as 4-by-8 inches, hexagons from 6 to 18 inches across and round pavers 2 feet or more in diameter. They may be a natural gray, or tinted almost any color. Some decorative concrete pavers are textured or

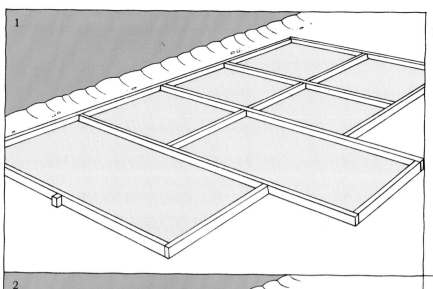

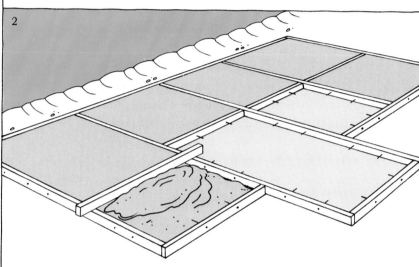

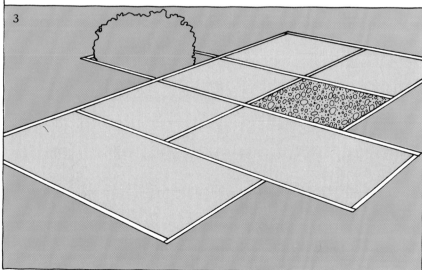

ADD-ON CONCRETE SLABS

1. *A design of rectangular grids for a concrete terrace divides the total area into small, easy-to-handle segments. Build the retaining forms of 2-by-4-inch redwood or other rot-resistant boards, or of lumber pressure-treated with a wood preservative. Set these forms on a bed of gravel 3 to 4 inches deep and brace them with stakes as necessary to prevent bulging. Any single section not reinforced with steel should be no larger than 16 square feet—4 by 4 feet. The maximum amount of concrete one person can handle conveniently in one day when working alone is about 15 cubic feet.*

2. *Working on one section at a time, pour the concrete, strike it off and smooth it, following the procedure shown on page 40. Drive 3-inch galvanized nails through the sides of the form boards at 1-foot intervals, so the concrete slab will be bonded to the wooden grid once it has hardened. Use a trowel or a mason's edger to round off the top corners of each slab. Protect the top edges of the wooden form boards from concrete stains by covering them with masking tape.*

3. *You can finish the surfaces of the concrete section with a rough-textured exposed aggregate (right center) or with a dust-on powdered tint of color, applied while the concrete is still damp. A wooden grid design permits future expansion. Plantings, such as the boxed-in bush at left, can be incorporated into your design.*

have pebbles cast into their surfaces, giving the effect of a brushed or exposed-aggregate concrete.

If you prize a natural look in your garden, quarried stones are hard to beat. Though they are more expensive than other pavers, their durability may justify the extra cost. If you live near a quarry, you may be able to buy them at a competitive price.

FLAGSTONES AS FLOORING

Flagstones—large flat pieces of shale, sandstone, granite or other evenly stratified rock—are available in random, irregular pieces (tricky to put together even if you enjoy jigsaw puzzles) or in rectangular pieces sawed to various sizes from 6 inches square to slabs 4 feet or more on a side. Colors range from gray, blue, red and green to almost black, depending on the kind of rock and where it was quarried. If you plan to lay flagstones directly on soil or sand, they should be 1½ to 2 inches thick. Stones that are thinner, particularly the fragile slate that is often mistaken for flagstone, may settle unevenly and crack under pressure unless secured with mortar on top of a concrete bed.

Many gardeners use flagstones to surface a badly worn patch of lawn. Flagstones also can be used to make a comfortable stepping-stone path if they are set close enough to each other so you will not have to negotiate them as though you were leaping onto boulders in a mountain stream. The width of your path is also important: 18 inches will be satisfactory for a little-used trail, but a width of 4 to 6 feet is necessary for a path that will allow two people to walk comfortably side by side.

To make a flagstone terrace or walk, position the stones and dig around each with a shovel to mark its outline. Set the stones aside and dig just deeply enough so the stones will be flush with the ground when they are replaced. To provide better drainage and minimize frost heaving, you can dig deeper and shovel in a 2- to 3-inch layer of coarse sand under each stone.

PAVINGS THAT POUR

Other kinds of hard paving, such as asphalt and concrete, are poured in place. Asphalt is inexpensive, but it is messy to work with and has a slick, blacktop look even when it is colored. Most gardeners use it only for driveways and have it professionally installed from a hot-mix truck. Fixed earth, which is a mixture of soil and cement, is another inexpensive paving material, but it looks like barren, hard-packed dirt.

The most durable, versatile and widely used poured paving is concrete. Placing and finishing it is heavy work that must be done correctly. If you have a large area of ground that needs to be paved, you probably will want to turn the job over to a professional, then sit down and watch. But if you can call on a helper or two to stand by for the critical pouring process, and if you can break the job down into small, manageable segments, you can save a good deal of money by doing it yourself.

Concrete, a mixture of portland cement, sand, gravel and water, is sold in several ways. For small jobs, like making a few steppingstones or lining a small garden pool, you can buy sacks of dry ready-mix. All you need do is add water and stir. For medium-sized jobs, such as surfacing a small sitting area or anchoring fence posts in concrete, you can save money by buying the portland cement, sand and gravel separately and mixing them with water in a wheelbarrow or a rented power mixer designed for home use. If you are working on a large area, you can do the preparatory excavating and leveling yourself, then have the concrete delivered, ready to

DRESSING UP CONCRETE

1. *To give wet concrete a smooth and level surface, trowel it with a wood float. Sweep the float back and forth in wide arcs with its face flat on the surface. As the slab hardens the float marks will gradually disappear.*

2. *Drawing a stiff-bristled push broom across wet concrete produces a textured and grooved nonskid surface. When the concrete is stiff but still workable, pull the broom in parallel sweeps across the slab, adjusting downward pressure on the bristles to make grooves as deep as you like.*

3. *Using a push broom and a fine spray from a garden hose, you can expose the small round stones of the gravel aggregate in wet concrete. For a uniform effect, you may need to scatter extra stones on the surface, using a wood float to press them down. Then wash excess concrete from the tops of the stones.*

4. *A stamping pad imprints a brick design on the surface of wet concrete. You can speed the work by renting two pads, available at masonry-supply stores, and leapfrogging them across the slab in rows. Use a hand tamper to press the pads down evenly.*

use, in a transit-mix truck. Most companies that supply concrete to builders will deliver ready-mixed concrete to do-it-yourself gardeners if the order is for at least 1 cubic yard.

One thrifty Minnesota handyman keeps several hinged wooden forms on hand for casting paving blocks with concrete left over from larger projects. "With the kind of weather we have around here, I have to replace several cracked blocks every spring," he explains. "It's nice to have extras on hand."

Poorly mixed concrete will doom the success of any project. If you use ready-mix, add the precise amount of water specified on the sack, thoroughly mixed to yield a product that is neither too wet, which would be structurally weak, nor too stiff and hard to work. If you start from scratch, a good concrete recipe calls for 1½ parts

SCREEDS FOR SMOOTHING

1. *To build a screed board for leveling gravel or sand, cut a 2-by-4 to fit easily inside the wooden frame in which you will spread the fill. Set this board on edge and nail a piece of scrap lumber to each end, so that the screed will ride on the top of the frame. A concave screed board will shape a concrete walk with a crown so it will shed water. Nail metal straps to the centers of a rigid 2-by-4 and a more flexible 2-by-2. Between their ends, wedge 1-inch dowels or other scraps to bow out the lower board. Add two more metal braces near the ends to make a solid striking board.*

2. *Set the screed board on top of a wooden frame that you have partly filled with drainage gravel or sand. Standing in the excavated bed, pull the screed board toward you, adding extra fill in low places as you go. Tamp the bed, then screed once again before you lay bricks or pour any concrete.*

3. *With the aid of a helper, work the concave screed board across the surface of the fresh concrete to compact and shape the slab. Use a small stick to push large pieces of gravel beneath the surface. Zigzagging the board as you draw it toward you makes the task easier.*

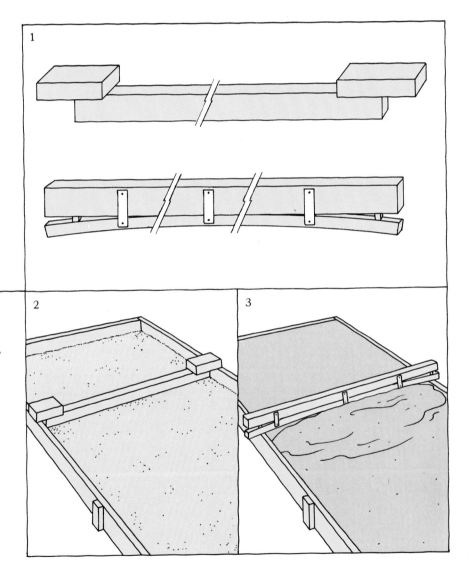

cement, 3⅓ parts builder's sand, 4½ parts gravel or crushed stone and 1 part water (page 35).

Concrete used in a climate where the ground is subject to freezing and thawing also needs an air-entraining agent; its microscopic bubbles, dispersed through the mix, act as tiny relief valves to prevent freezing moisture from cracking the finished work. This eliminates the need for costly, time-consuming repairs.

For strong, durable concrete in any climate, do not neglect proper curing. The binding together of the cement, sand and gravel depends on a chemical process called hydration, which needs not only water but warmth to take place and continues well after the concrete itself has been poured; temperatures below 50° impede the process and if the material ever dries out hydration stops completely and cannot be started again. As soon as the surface has been finished and is hard enough to resist imprints, usually a few hours at most, wet it down thoroughly with a fine spray from a garden hose, cover it with burlap, canvas or straw—even old blankets—and keep the covering in place and constantly moist for a week. Wide rolls of polyethylene black plastic sheeting or waterproof building paper can be used instead, and if they are held down tightly at the edges with bricks or boards, they will keep the concrete's own moisture in.

Finally, you do not need to leave the surface with a white, raw look. You can add colored dusting pigments before the concrete hardens and use a wooden float to make the surface smooth enough to double as a dance floor. If you prefer a rougher texture, brush the concrete while it is still soft with a stiff broom. If you pour plain concrete and decide later to improve its appearance, there are stains and paints made especially for that purpose. Or you can use a concrete slab as a foundation for the later application of brick, flagstone, slate or tile.

Garden steps, too, can be made of concrete, poured into rigid wooden forms, or of materials as diverse as precast concrete blocks, railroad ties or wood planking. The more sloping or irregular your garden site, the greater the role that steps will play. The lay of the land will largely determine the layout of your steps, but wide steps with a gradual rise are best anywhere in a garden. Indoors, many stairs have 6-inch risers (the height between steps) and treads that are 12 inches deep (from front to back). This should be the maximum steepness outdoors. Better are steps with 5-inch risers and 15-inch treads, 4-inch risers and 18-inch treads, even 3-inch risers and 24-inch treads.

Some landscape architects determine step proportions with a standard formula: twice the height of the riser plus the depth of the

THE CURING PROCESS

EASY STEPS TO TAKE

BUILDING A MODULAR DECK

1. *To assemble wooden deck modules 24 inches square, nail evenly spaced rows of surface boards to rot-resistant supports. To ensure that the modules are square, build them within a squared-up frame made of scrap lumber, nailed down so that it will not shift, with inside dimensions equal to the size of the modules. Use scraps of wood ¼ inch thick as spacers between the surface boards (inset).*

2. *Drive three nails through the ends of each surface board into its support, staggering the nails and blunting the points to prevent splitting the wood.*

3. *On the ground, lay out a rectangular site for the deck by stringing lines between stakes, making right-angle corners with the 3-4-5 method (page 58). Then excavate the site to a depth of about 6 inches to accommodate a drainage bed for the deck. Tamp the ground, making it as level as possible.*

4. *A cross section of the drainage bed for the deck shows a 3-inch layer of gravel covered with a 4-inch layer of sand. Rake and tamp the sand until the surface of the drainage bed is firm and level. To prevent weeds from growing through the deck, treat the soil beneath it with weed killer, or lay perforated sheets of asphalt builder's paper over the drainage bed (page 33), and cover the sheets with a thin layer of sand.*

5. *Assemble the deck, module by module, in a parquet pattern. Tamp each module firmly into the sand, keeping the edges even.*

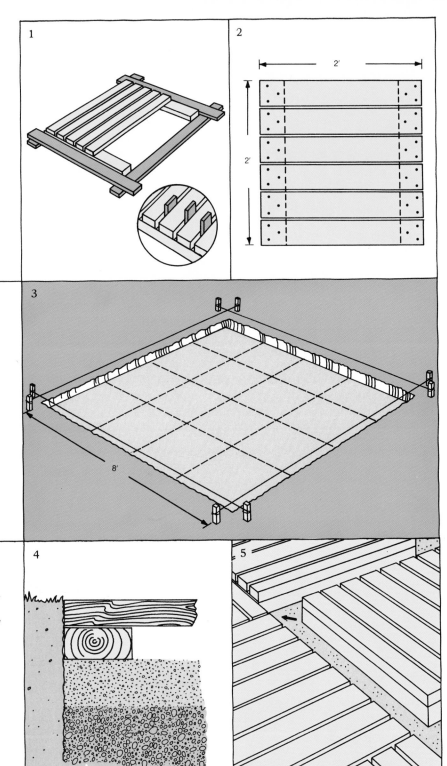

tread should equal 26 inches. Thus, a 5-inch riser, multiplied by two and subtracted from 26 would prescribe a 16-inch-deep tread. As for width, 3 feet is sufficient for lightly used steps, but a width of 4 or 5 feet is desirable for heavier traffic and for safety on steps used frequently for moving plants, wheelbarrows and lawn mowers from one level to another.

For raised decks the most widely used flooring material probably is wood. Popularized in recent years by California hill dwellers, such decks have become commonplace in suburban communities from Tacoma to Tallahassee, on level sites as well as those that slope. In addition to being adaptable to almost any style of garden, wood is light and easy to work with, blends well with other construction materials and offers an attractive nonskid surface that is comfortable to the touch.

Paving units made of wood and set directly on the ground will last for many years if the wood is rot-resistant or treated with a preservative (page 15). Blocks 4 to 6 inches thick, set end grain up and closely butted together, are suitable for edging plant beds or paving garden paths. Wood rounds cut from tree trunks can serve as steppingstones along woodland paths or as decorative patterns in terraces of gravel or crushed stone.

If you incorporate wood pavers into your garden design, lay them in a drainage bed of 2 or 3 inches of sand, gravel or crushed stone. By filling the irregular spaces between wood rounds with more of the same materials, or with bark chunks or wood chips, you can enhance the wood's beauty. But avoid using such wood paving in areas that are heavily shaded and constantly moist. The wood will rot and its surface may become slippery and dangerous to the safety of casual strollers.

The most durable and useful wood paving is spaced planking raised above the ground. Raising wood even a few inches from the earth ensures good drainage and air circulation; such decking is uniform and resilient, and it will dry quickly after rain. These low decks are useful if you want to bring an outdoor living area level with an inside room, eliminating an awkward step down.

On irregular ground, decks do away with the need for expensive grading, filling and retaining walls. Instead, the heights of supports beneath the deck can be varied to fit the topography. And once you have built a basic deck, you can add railings, built-in seating and storage space, or even leave holes in the decking so trees can grow through it from below. With imaginative design you can make your deck, in the words of noted landscape architect Thomas Church, "a treehouse for adults."

WOOD DECKS AND PAVERS

SMOOTHING HILL AND DALE

Decks: varied, versatile and inviting

A garden expands when it is equipped with a wooden deck. The potential for outdoor living increases as the new space invites people to be convivial, or to sit quietly in contemplation of nature.

Endlessly versatile, a wooden deck can be designed for virtually any garden site, with but slight disturbance to soil and plantings, and without the costly grading and filling that so often accompany the construction of a terrace of brick or stone. Still, any deck must be placed with care.

An example of artful placement and construction is offered by the deck illustrated opposite and on the cover. The slope on which the huge California live oak stands was too steep for walking or for sitting, and the ground could not be reshaped without risk of damage to the tree's sensitive root system. A wooden deck was the answer. Built on two levels to accommodate the tree's branching structure and supported by concrete footings and wooden posts, the deck can hold 20 guests comfortably, yet it does not crowd the magnificent old tree. Ample margin is left for the oak's girth to enlarge and for its four trunks to sway in the wind without chafing against the deck frame. Edges of the deck are well within the tree's drip line, so there is no interference with the water supply to feeder roots; if a tree's drip line is covered, it may need supplementary irrigation.

Like a tree, any deck adds a strong design element to a garden. The monotony of a perfectly level yard can be broken with geometrical patterns introduced by a deck. A deck can even create new levels, and new interest, with a change in its surface planes. It can also enfold and unify disparate elements in a garden, bringing scattered plantings into harmony with one another.

And like a tree, a deck becomes more beautiful with the passing years. "Most gardens are too young," a noted landscape architect wrote. Old gardens in America are the treasures of very few; most gardeners must struggle with raw newness. But in the sun and rain, a wooden deck quickly acquires a patina of age—with many years of sturdy and useful life still ahead.

A railed deck has made this shady garden corner a favored place for friends to gather. Low-voltage lights set in the California live oak provide evening illumination.

Scaling a 15-foot slope from poolside to a larger deck above, these layered decks neatly screen a swimming-pool filter unit, housed under the middle deck behind the topiary tree. The decks and a built-in picnic table at right welcome diners.

46

Stacked decks to sculpt slopes

Stacked decks not only ease the climb up a steep garden embankment, they sculpt the slope into striking new shapes. Combinations of decks and stairs form paths with way-stops en route that one designer calls viewing nodes—places where the path turns in such a way that the eye is led to a new garden view. The small decks also tend to break a party crush into small conversation groups.

Fitted carefully among the tall oaks that surround a home in upper Michigan, a three-tier series of decks leads down to a lakeshore, just beyond the deck in the foreground. The informal lines of the decks echo the casual house architecture.

Walkways by the water

For a house that is near the water, decks have many uses—as a means of access to the water's edge, as footpaths that permit the tending of shoreline plantings, as subtle and unobtrusive markers for the borders of valuable property. But their greatest value lies in their ability to unify a house, garden and shoreline into a harmonious whole.

For example, the house at the left is located on a comparatively small lot on a lagoon off San Francisco Bay. The shore had little utility until the two decks that reach toward the water and frame a garden made it a place where friends often gather.

Within a flowing pattern of walkways and decks nestle four kinds of juniper, a Japanese black pine, strawberries, blue fescue grass and other plantings set amid fieldstones. Like arms, the sitting areas wrap around this garden and reach toward the lagoon beyond.

Treehouse for adults

Decks can be set amid trees at almost any height, provided there is some way to cantilever or support them. On a steep, wooded hillside, a deck such as the one in the two views at left and below can create living space literally at treetop level. Such a deck offers panoramic vistas unattainable before, making sitting and dining outdoors exhilarating experiences. With shelter added, the deck becomes an adult treehouse for all seasons.

Added onto a concrete terrace (left), this wooden-floored, steel-railed deck increases outdoor living space by some 1,000 square feet. It provides spectacular views of the San Fernando Valley. At night, guests gather around the stone fire pit (center) while lights twinkle far below.

Perched breathtakingly on a precipice, a deck nestles in the very top of an acacia tree (opposite). Heavy wooden posts underpin the structure, and slatted boards overhead provide shade against the afternoon sun. This deck also incorporates an ancient pear tree growing near the house below.

A greenhouse in the sky

On a bare and plunging slope, the landscaping choices are few. Planting ivy is one. Building a deck that soars out of the incline into the sky is another—a way of creating usable space where none existed and, in effect, buying land in the sky.

Here, one gardener has put his midair land to very imaginative cultivation. He has erected a hydroponic, electrically heated greenhouse where he grows vegetables year round. The side cabinet flanking the deck has a metal top for potting plants; below is storage space for tools, planting mixes and fertilizers. Bank plantings receive waste water from the greenhouse.

A stairway of railroad ties leads to a spectacularly located small greenhouse. Pfitzer junipers border the steps, while a clump of Acacia latifolia edges the deck. Many visitors have admired this deck and greenhouse, but, lacking the rarified location, few can hope to emulate it.

Ins and outs of fences and walls 3

From prehistoric times, when man-the-hunter built rude barricades of thorns to keep wild animals away, through thousands of years of building walls and fences to keep livestock in and trespassers out, barriers of one sort or another have provided privacy and protection. In modern gardens, walls and fences serve many purposes well beyond these, from screening bashful sun bathers to extending the apparent size of a house.

Low walls can mark off parts of a garden according to how each area is used, provide interesting changes of level, double as benches for casual sitting, or lift plants above ground level so they can be tended without bending and stooping. Higher dividers are used to screen off unsightly service areas, garbage cans, compost heaps and vegetable or cutting gardens that have passed their prime.

Along property lines, fences and walls can provide privacy, reduce noise and wind velocity, form sun traps that extend the use of a garden in cool weather and serve as backdrops for flowers, shrubs and climbing vines. As a safety device, fencing can confine children and pets, or keep them from falling into a swimming pool.

There are almost as many kinds of fences and walls as there are people to build them. Among the oldest, and still most widely used, are boundary fences. In 18th Century America, when wood was plentiful but nails were scarce, boundary fences were made from long, hand-split tree trunks simply stacked at angles in a zigzag pattern to make self-supporting barriers. These so-called rail fences contained the landowner's livestock and put others on notice that he had staked his claim to the enclosed area.

As timber became more valuable and property lines more precisely defined, the kinks in the zigzag fence gradually disappeared. The split rails were stacked one on another in a straight line and the ends were held together by pairs of posts set firmly in the ground. From this evolved the familiar post-and-rail fence: single

A Revolutionary era wall skillfully constructed of fieldstones without mortar makes an impressive backdrop for a contemporary herb garden in Connecticut in which yellow hollyhocks also grow.

posts with holes in them to receive the ends of the rails. Finally, as machine-milled lumber became available, it replaced the hand-hewn parts. These post-and-board fences, still seen surrounding many a farm pasture and suburban yard, led to the picket fence (*page 62*) and to all manner of contemporary designs.

RAISING A BARRICADE

While boundary fences today are usually more esthetic than utilitarian, security fences are strictly practical. Among the most effective is the chain-link fence, with its unmistakable "no trespassing" look. Only a professional can install a chain-link fence properly, but an imaginative gardener can do many things to soften its appearance. One Washington, D.C., handyman, whose apartment terrace is separated from a parking lot by a chain-link fence, wove the slats from several old venetian blinds through the fence links. The resulting latticework blocks an undesirable view but allows ample ventilation for a border of peonies and pansies.

Aware of the appearance problem, manufacturers of chain-link fences offer cap rails to soften the jagged top edge, plastic-coated mesh in unobtrusive green or black, and slats of wood or plastic to weave through the links as the Washington gardener did. You can also lash panels of canvas or reed screening to such a fence. But the most effective way to modify the harsh look of a chain-link fence is

STRETCHING WIRE-MESH FENCING

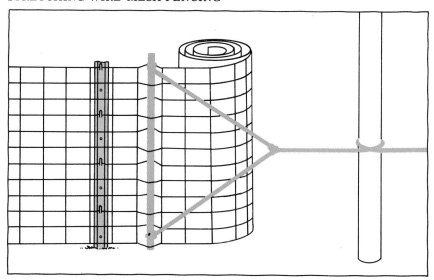

To stretch wire fencing, run a stick—a broom handle will do—through the standing mesh just past a fence post. Then attach a rope to both ends of the stick so it can be pulled evenly. Wrap the other end of the rope around a stationary object such as a tree or a firmly braced corner fence post. Tighten the rope; if necessary, use a block and tackle. For safety's sake, do not pull with a car. When the mesh feels springy to the touch, fasten it to the post nearest the stretching-stick, then release the rope.

to camouflage it with a dense, fast-growing vine—perhaps a Boston ivy, honeysuckle or Virginia creeper—making it look like a hedge.

An alternative to chain-link fencing is welded wire mesh, which has a more tailored rectangular pattern. It can be set into wooden frames to form unobtrusive low or high fences. To discourage climbers, use mesh with a narrow vertical dimension of 2 inches or less so toeholds will be difficult.

Between the extremes of decoration and security, there are many reasons to build a fence. For most homeowners, particularly those with cramped urban lots, privacy is paramount: they would rather not share all the details of their leisure hours with neighbors and passersby. A privacy fence should be at least 6 feet high, solid enough to screen undesirable viewing, yet not so solid that it will prevent cooling breezes from penetrating on a sweltering day.

Some homeowners rush out to buy instant privacy in the form of prefabricated fence sections, made either of flat boards butted solidly together or of saplings or half-round poles joined to form a modern version of the frontier stockade fence. Such fences unquestionably provide privacy, but they can present a formidable appearance that suggests all too well their rude and defensive origins.

A better and more economical solution is to build your own privacy fence to perform exactly the role you require. Several variations of the basic post-and-board fence are shown in the encyclopedia *(pages 116-119)*. Among these are the basketweave fence, made of thin boards bent around vertical or horizontal spacers; fences with horizontal or vertical louvers set at an angle; and fences built with a board-and-board design.

The board-and-board fence, one of the easiest to build, consists of vertical boards nailed alternately on opposite sides of a simple wooden frame. A board-and-board fence presents a pleasing appearance on both sides and the deep shadow pattern it creates provides privacy with ventilation. A board-and-board fence can be built with less lumber than most other privacy fences and requires no complex joints. In a long fence, the repetitive pattern can be broken by nailing alternating sections in a horizontal pattern (although this permits easy climbing).

Surprisingly, a board-and-board fence—or any fence with a partly open structure—is usually more effective than a solid fence in shielding a sitting area from wind. The openings diffuse wind, while a solid fence often creates a swirling eddy that draws fast-moving air down from the top of the fence onto the lee side.

If you want to build a fence or wall on or near your property line and you are not sure exactly where that line is, by all means

THE WORLD EXCLUDED

BOARD-AND-BOARD DESIGN

have your land resurveyed. In most communities, your neighbor's side of any barrier exactly on the property line belongs to him—to modify, maintain or let go to ruin. You will certainly want to discuss the fence with him beforehand to avoid any misunderstanding or ill will. And you may be better off erecting your fence 12 to 18 inches inside the line. This gives you undisputed ownership and allows space for repairs and repainting without trespassing. Even if you set back the fence, however, choose a "good neighbor" design and keep it properly maintained on both sides.

PRECISION PLACEMENT

Once you have reconciled your fence design with local codes and with neighbors, you can plot its exact placement. A simple way to make sure the fence is properly located and of the right height is to tie a length of twine to a couple of long poles and have two helpers move this rig around the yard. As you stand or sit in key areas, sight across the top of the string as your helpers adjust it up, down and sideways. Newspapers folded over the string will help you to visualize the view when the fence is erected. After experimenting, you may find that you need a higher or lower fence than you had thought, or that only some sections need be of a closed design.

The first step in building a fence is to locate the exact positions of the end and corner posts, drive a stake at each post location and

RIGHT ANGLES FOR A RECTANGLE

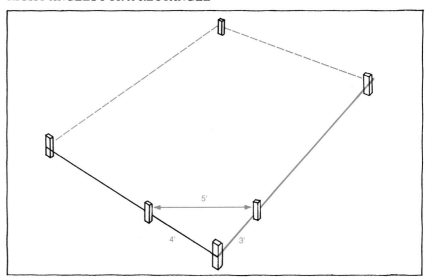

To set stakes at right angles marking the corner of a plant bed, a terrace or a yard being fenced, use a 3-4-5 triangle. Mark one side with two stakes and a string (red line). Stretch and stake a second string (black line) at an approximate right angle to the first.

Drive a stake just outside the first line 3 feet from the corner and another 4 feet from the corner on the adjacent side. Tie a third string (blue line) to these stakes. Adjust the second string until the diagonal is 5 feet long; the corner will be a 90° angle.

tie a piece of string taut between the stakes. The corners of most residential lots form right angles, but your angle may not be precisely 90°. You can check the angle with a carpenter's square, but a surer method is to use another piece of string to form a so-called 3-4-5 triangle. To make this triangle, attach the third piece of string to the two pieces already forming the corner, tying it 3 feet from the corner stake on one side and 4 feet from the stake on the other. If this diagonal string (the hypotenuse of the triangle) measures exactly 5 feet, the corner angle is the desired 90°.

After you have squared up the corner, drive stakes along the twine to mark the positions of intervening posts. Most wooden garden fences are built with posts 8 feet apart and use crosspieces of standard 8-foot lumber, though a solid fence of heavy lumber or one subjected to strong winds is better supported every 4 or 6 feet. If you end with an odd length that upsets the fence's symmetry, you can divide the run into equal sections and cut all horizontal pieces to fit, or you can fill the odd gap with a gate.

On some sites, natural or man-made obstacles may prevent laying out a fence in a straight line. If a tree is directly on the fence line, stop the fence short of the trunk on either side, leaving a few inches of space to allow continued growth. Never use a tree as a fence post; as the tree grows, it will push the fence out of line. Worse, driving nails into a tree will open pathways for infection.

If you build a fence on sloping or irregular ground, you can keep the top of the fence level by making some posts longer than others. On steeper sites, sections of the fence can step down like a flight of stairs.

Most garden fences are built on frames of 4-by-4 posts connected near the top and bottom with horizontal pieces called stringers or rails. The most critical part of fence building is getting this framework solidly in place and perfectly in line. For stability, fence posts usually are sunk into the ground at least one third their total length. Thus, a fence 6 feet high would be built with 9-foot posts. In areas with extreme winter cold, posts long enough to reach below the frost line will be more stable. All posts should be of wood that has been pressure-treated with a preservative, or of heartwood of a naturally rot-resistant species like redwood or cedar.

In well-drained, stable soils, fence posts can be set in postholes without concrete. Dig the holes with a screw auger or a two-handled posthole digger of the clamshell type; those dug with a shovel are too large and will need a lot of backfilling and compacting to keep the posts from wobbling. To provide drainage at the base of each post, the point most vulnerable to rot, place a flat stone at the bottom of

OBSTACLE COURSES

SETTING A FENCE POST

each hole or line it with a 2- to 3-inch layer of gravel or crushed rock. Then put the post in the hole, using a carpenter's level to get it vertical. While a helper holds the post, shovel in 2 or 3 more inches of gravel, tamp it with the end of a 2-by-4 *(page 32)*, then add soil and tamp until the hole is full, checking the post with a level every few inches to make sure it remains vertical. When the hole is full, mound up earth around the post so surface water will drain away.

For more solid footings for gateposts and corner posts and for those subject to frost heaving or strong wind, you can supplement the earth and gravel fill with one or more collars of concrete. The technique of setting a post in concrete without creating a pocket that invites rot at the bottom of the post is shown on page 66.

ADDING THE RAILS

When all of the posts are evenly in place, mark the position of the rails by tacking one string near the tops of the posts and another near the ground. With a helper keeping a lower rail level, toenail it in place by hammering galvanized nails diagonally through its sides into the post. For a stronger joint, you can toenail the rail through the top edge, keeping the rail in place by resting it on small wooden cleats nailed to the posts *(page 10)*.

Top rails can simply be laid across two post tops and nailed onto them. A stronger fence can be made by using top rails that span three posts and meet at the center of every third post. In either case, the top rail serves the important function of keeping moisture from soaking into the tops of the posts. If you do leave post tops exposed, cap them with metal or bevel them slightly so moisture will run off.

SPACED SLATS OR BOARDS

Once the posts and rails are in place, you are ready to nail on the slats, pickets or boards that complete the design of your fence. The work will go quickly if you use a spacer board, made from a length of scrap lumber cut to the width of the gaps with a cleat nailed to one end to form a T. After you have nailed on the first picket or board, hang the spacer board's cleat on the top rail, hold the spacer tight against the first board, and nail the second board next to it. Move the spacer for each new board.

As a general rule, only the fence posts should touch the ground. If you want to exclude small animals, you can tack wire mesh along the bottom rail. The fence can be finished with a coat of preservative stain or with one or more coats of exterior latex or oil-based paint. White is a safe traditional color for fences.

If you have a problem that a board fence will not solve, you can adapt the basic frame to hold panels of exterior-grade plywood, plastic, glass or some other material *(page 119)*.

Despite their myriad uses and charms, fences probably will never completely replace walls, the oldest and most durable of man-made dividers. Gardens and walls have gone together for thousands of years, combining permanence, privacy and dignity.

The most venerable walls are made of stone. Building a stone wall has always been an arduous craft, requiring not only patience and a strong back but a keen eye for compositon and accurate fitting. For most homeowners, a stone wall is only an object to admire. But for a few, among them gardener Charles Fenyvesi, there is great satisfaction in building such a wall.

"It is glorious how well a dry wall stands up to children and weather and time," Fenyvesi wrote in *The New York Times*. "Walls define space. They declare where the children's realm ends and the flowers' begins. They grant one level to tall lilies; another to creeping phlox and portulaca. . . .

"I mix shapes and sizes and I use everything that comes my way: chewed-up pieces of concrete, slag, the fragment of a colonade. I believe a broken brick looks good next to gray volcanic pebbles. I marry smooth black slate to rough, white rock crystal. . . .

"Building a wall, I remember the terraced hills of Jerusalem, Java and China. I ponder the symmetries of Islam's walled gardens. I daydream about stone towers overlooking a plain that invading foreigners cross."

FENCES THAT FOLLOW A SLOPE

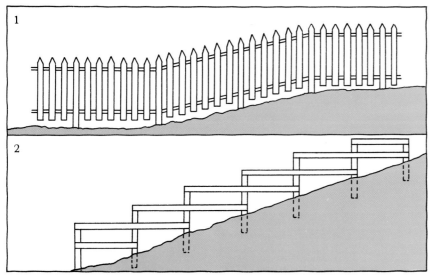

1. *On a gradual slope, you can put up fencing that follows the natural contour of the land by setting posts of identical height at regular intervals and letting the rails parallel the incline. Use a carpenter's level to keep posts and pickets vertical.*

2. *On a steeper slope, a fence may be stepped down in sections by connecting vertical posts with horizontal rails—again, use a carpenter's level. Where the slope varies, set posts at different heights, but keep the rail length constant.*

Even if walls do not evoke such a vivid sense of romance for you, they are useful in defining garden areas and changing levels, preventing soil erosion and containing raised planting beds.

For the novice builder there are many widely available masonry materials that are easier to work with than stone, including bricks and precast concrete blocks. A low edging to hold a plant bed can be made simply by setting paving bricks on end so the tops protrude a few inches above the soil level. A popular decorative variation of this mortarless edging requires only that you tilt bricks in a trench at a 45° angle *(page 34)*.

WALLS TO LIFT PLANTS

Not much harder to build are walls 1 to 3 feet high; gardeners are turning in increasing numbers to raised plant beds within such walls, because they make strong patterns, they raise plants to a level where they are easily tended, and they provide containers for a rich planting mix regardless of the quality of the soil beneath. Moreover, such raised planting beds protect vegetables and flowers from children, pets and pests. A Louisville, Kentucky, couple lost more than 100 tulip bulbs one year to mice and moles who found them easy pickings in an in-ground bed. The following year, with the bulbs ensconced in a raised planter, the couple lost not a single one.

The simplest raised bed can be built of 2-by-8 or 2-by-10 boards of rot-resistant or treated lumber, set edgewise an inch or two in the ground, nailed together at the corners and filled with soil. For a more permanent structure, lay one or more tiers of railroad ties or landscape timbers around the bed and join them at the inside corners with galvanized angle irons. Ties can be further stabilized by drilling holes through them, about 3 feet apart, and pounding lengths of

(continued on page 66)

The picket's ordered grace

Nearly half of the seven miles of fences in Williamsburg, the painstakingly restored capital of colonial Virginia, are picket fences—pointed stakes 3 to 4½ feet tall spaced evenly along horizontal rails strung between taller posts. The continuing popularity of such fences lies not so much in their functional role as in the decorativeness of their orderly and rhythmic vertical lines, punctuated at regular intervals by posts. Not the sort of fence for anyone craving privacy, the low and open pickets invite public appraisal of the architecture and gardens they enclose.

Though selected to complement colonial architecture, Williamsburg's fences suggest the adaptability of pickets to almost any building style. The Victorians, in fact, narrowed their pickets to simulate wrought iron or cut the edges of broad pickets to echo the gingerbread cornices on their houses. The picket fence is as traditional as any structure can be, but it continues to evolve; one contemporary architect specifies pickets made of round dowels and painted earth colors instead of the familiar white.

Affluent colonists discreetly expressed their taste with graceful fences like this one of gently undulating pickets.

HIGH-LOW PICKETS

ARCHED PICKETS

DIAMOND-CUT PICKETS

Colonial conformity

The lines of picket fencing in Williamsburg harmoniously merge the flat public commons they face with the well-kept gardens and tidy colonial homes behind them. The town's uniformity is deliberate. Williamsburg's planners decreed by law that all houses occupy plots of at least a half acre, stand 6 feet back from the street, and be "paled in" to keep the livestock that grazed on the commons from nibbling at the tender shoots of vegetables in kitchen gardens. Wood was readily available in the young colony, and fences of pales (now called pickets or stakes) were easy to construct from hand-sawed lumber, boards torn roughly from logs (rived pickets) or even with plain, easily gathered, bark-covered saplings.

ROUNDED PICKETS

ARROWHEAD PICKETS

SPADE-SHAPED PICKETS

SPEARHEAD PICKETS

ANGLE-CUT PICKETS

POINTED PICKETS

STEPPED PICKETS

FLAT-TOP PICKETS

DOUBLE SAW-TOOTH PICKETS

TRIPLE SAW-TOOTH PICKETS

galvanized pipe through the holes and into the ground beneath.

You can also build a low retaining structure by piling up rough stones without mortar to form a rudimentary but serviceable New England-style dry wall. For stability, set the stones at a slight downward angle toward the inside of the wall and slope the wall back at least an inch for every foot of height.

A stone retaining wall higher than 3 feet is more difficult. It requires a solid foundation, or footing, usually of poured concrete. The wall itself generally must be built of mortared masonry or poured concrete, with weep holes to relieve water pressure and lateral members called "dead men" to anchor the structure into the slope behind. The construction of such a wall is best left in the hands of a professional builder.

LAYING BRICKS OR BLOCKS

Many less complex walls can be built with bricks or concrete blocks. Brick is as handsome in walls as it is in paving, and there are several decorative kinds of concrete block that can be used to create stunning grillwork effects.

For many garden uses, from low sitting or retaining walls to higher utility or privacy enclosures, a wall of ordinary concrete block is quite adequate. Blocks are more economical and go up faster than stone or brick; one hollow-core concrete block takes up roughly the

FIRM FOUNDATIONS FOR FENCE POSTS

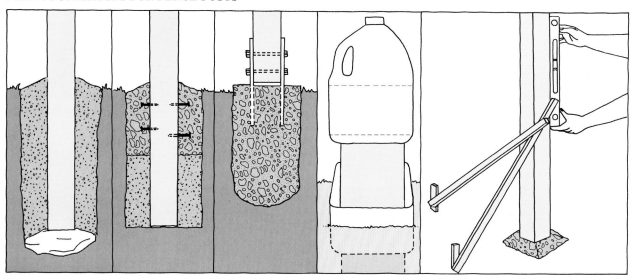

Fence posts may be set in the ground with tamped earth (left) or held more firmly with concrete collars (right). Nails in the posts anchor them to the concrete. For good drainage, set each post on a large stone and mound up the fill at ground level.

For a firmer fence-post foundation, sink an H-shaped metal post anchor in concrete. Fasten the post to the anchor with bolts (left). To make a neat concrete collar, use a band cut from a plastic jug to shape the wet concrete (right).

If you are setting a post without a helper, tamp enough earth around it to hold it steady. Use a carpenter's level to align the post, then brace it temporarily with scrap lumber and stakes. Keep checking the level as you add the fill around the post.

same space as 16 bricks, though its 40- to 50-pound weight should be reckoned with (somewhat lighter cinder blocks and other lightweight blocks of 25 to 30 pounds are also available). Nor does a block wall have to look like the rear of a factory; it can be painted or stuccoed white or an attractive pastel color and further graced with plantings such as climbing vines. A solid, blank appearance, moreover, can be avoided by choosing specially sculptured or textured blocks, or open screen or grillwork blocks. The effect of screen blocks can also be obtained with ordinary blocks: simply lay all or some on edge to expose their hollow cores in patterns that will admit light, breeze and view without totally sacrificing privacy.

Building a low-to-medium-height wall of concrete block does not take a high degree of skill, and the techniques are essentially the same if you want to try brick instead. A typical hollow-core block has nominal dimensions of 8 by 8 by 16 inches but is actually enough smaller to allow for a ⅜-inch mortar joint between blocks. To complete ends and corners there are also half blocks and corner blocks with one end flat where it will be exposed; for special patterns you can also buy half-height and partition blocks measuring 4 by 8 by 16 inches; for topping finished walls with copings, you can use solid, coreless cap blocks 2 to 4 inches thick.

Unless you are building a very low wall in a frost-free area in stable soil, you will probably need a foundation at least 6 inches deep and a foot wide, deeper if you have to go below the frost line so the wall will not heave and crack. If the wall is not an extensive one, you can buy sacks of ready-mix concrete, add water and shovel it into a prepared trench that is reinforced with a lining of steel mesh. If the wall is more than 4 feet high or must hold back a heavy load of earth, it will need steel reinforcing rods ½ inch in diameter embedded every 4 feet in the foundation so they protrude about 2 feet in the air to anchor the concrete blocks. The reinforcing rods tie the wall to the concrete foundation for greater strength. Use a piece of board to smooth off the top of the concrete, keeping it straight with the help of a carpenter's level, stakes and string.

When the concrete has hardened, generally in a couple of days, lay out a test course of unmortared blocks, allowing ⅜-inch gaps for the joints; mark the ends and set the blocks aside. The sturdiest all-round way to lay up block or brick is the conventional running bond, in which the units overlap. You can get an elegant modern look, however, by using a stacked bond, in which all vertical as well as horizontal joints align, though you should imbed strips of galvanized metal hardware cloth or special Z-shaped wire ties in the horizontal joints to increase stability.

POURING THE FOUNDATION

Wet down the foundation with a hose and start laying the blocks from the ends inward, using a mortar made of 1 part masonry cement and 3 parts sand with just enough water added to yield a stiff mix that will not squeeze out of the joints under the weight of the blocks. Check frequently with the carpenter's level and a string stretched to mark the top of each course, tapping blocks with the handle of the trowel to get them in line. Tool the joints to a concave or V profile when they have hardened slightly, fill any cores containing reinforcing rods with a grout mix of cement and gravel and top off the wall with coping blocks. After the mortar joints have dried for a few days you can paint your wall with either exterior latex or masonry paint. The latter must be scrubbed into the wetted blocks with a wire brush but then becomes very durable; latex is almost as good and a lot easier to apply with a long-napped roller.

Wherever you build a fence or a wall, there are two final details to consider: access and compatible planting. If a garden path leads through a decorative barrier, you can just leave a gap. Such gaps, originally designed to permit the passage of a man but to stop farm animals, were common in rural America of the 19th Century, when they were called stiles or wickets. George Martin, the author of an 1887 book, *Fences, Gates and Bridges,* included this recommendation: "The opening in these stiles must be sufficient to allow a corpulent person to pass easily, even if a frisky bull is in uncomfortable proximity." But Martin also noted that calves, sheep, pigs and dogs could work their way through the most ingenious of ungated stiles. Therefore, stiles sometimes incorporated two short flights of stairs to permit a person easy passage over the top of the fence. It is not likely that you will be confining a frisky bull in your garden, but if the purpose of your wall is to obscure the view beyond, offset the sections on either side of the opening by about 3 feet and overlap them a foot or two.

GATEWAY TO THE GARDEN

Other kinds of walls and fences require some sort of gate for security or appearance. Any gate, particularly one on an entrance walk, should be a decorative focal point. Like an unclosed opening, it should be at least 3 feet wide and the gate should swing inward from hinges located on the right.

You can build a simple garden gate on a framework of 2-by-4s sheathed with pickets, boards or slats. The gateposts should be sunk 3 feet or more into the ground or anchored to a nearby wall so the gate will swing freely and not sag after repeated use.

For the gardener, one of the special joys of building a fence or wall is the opportunity to train many varieties of climbing plants to grow up, around and over it, casting lovely patterns of light and shadow. Clinging vines such as English ivy, winter creeper and climbing hydrangea, for example, will climb right up a brick or stone wall. Avoid growing vines on a wooden fence, however, since they may encourage algae and keep the wood damp, causing it to rot. It is also wise to avoid planting vigorous, heavy vines such as climbing roses or bittersweet on a lightweight fence. Unless you are willing to prune them back diligently, the plants will weigh heavily on the structure and may even pull it down.

The best vines to grow on a painted or stained wooden surface are those that twine as they climb—wisteria, for example—or those such as clematis that coil their tendrils around projections. For any vine, lightweight plastic-coated wire mesh attached to a wall or fence will serve as an inexpensive and virtually invisible trellis.

Fences and walls also make splendid backdrops for all manner of shrubs and flowers planted in front of them. Many tender plants that could not otherwise survive in northerly climates will thrive on the sunny side of a wall, sheltered from the wind. South-facing white walls or fences can bring spring bulbs and flowering shrubs into bloom weeks ahead of time. And for shade-and-moisture plants, from filmy ferns to spectacular tuberous begonias, the north side of a dark wall, under open sky, may be just right.

VINES THAT TWINE OR COIL

DRY STONE WALLS: STRONG AND STABLE

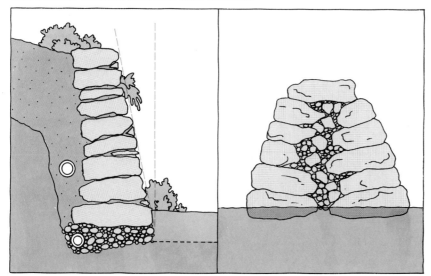

In a typical stone retaining wall built without mortar, the stones tilt upward at the front and the wall leans into the slope to forestall washouts. Additional drainage is provided by coarse gravel under the wall and by two courses of perforated draintiles.

A sturdy wall of fieldstones can be built in front and back courses that lean inward, with individual stones sloping slightly downward at the center so gravity helps hold the wall erect. Fill the middle space with an interlocking rubble of smaller stones.

Raising a roof for shelter or storage 4

There is no more pleasant place in a garden than a shady corner where you can while away an hour or two on a lazy summer afternoon. If you are fortunate enough to have a large shade tree in your backyard, you need only place a comfortable piece of lawn furniture beneath its leafy boughs. But if you are not so blessed, you can build your own shade exactly where you want it: a structure that may be a simple arbor covered with vines or an ornate gazebo like the ones that adorned so many Victorian gardens.

If, on the other hand, you have all the shade you need but are short of storage space, construction can solve that problem, too. There are many strictly utilitarian structures you can build, ranging from covered bins to hold tools or firewood to a potting shed or even a fully equipped work center where you can store tools, raise seedlings and start cuttings.

Of the many kinds of garden shelters, probably the most common—and among the easiest to build—is a terrace roof consisting of a simple framework of wooden posts, beams and rafters attached to a wall of the house *(page 73)*. Four-by-four posts are strong enough to support most terrace roofs, although unusually large structures or those that are built in snow country may require 4-by-6s. Check the requirements of your local building code; the structure may have to withstand heavy wind, not to mention your own weight as you build it.

The size of the beams, or horizontal supporting members, depends on the distance between posts. As a general rule, the depth of the beam in inches should equal the span of the beam in feet. Thus, a 4-by-4 beam can be expected to span 4 feet, while a 4-by-6 beam will span 6 feet. The size of the rafters, which rest across the beams, is also determined by the distance they span and the weight of the load they will have to support. Relative post, beam and rafter sizes are shown in the chart on page 150.

A wire enclosure supported by a skeleton of 2-by-4s protects the broccoli, peppers and other comestibles of a vegetable garden from marauding birds and animals. Posts are bolted where the top was added on.

If your building code permits, you can set roof posts directly in the ground, using wood that has been treated with a preservative or the naturally rot-resistant heartwood of cedar or redwood. Set each post at least 3 feet below grade, or below the greatest depth of winter frost, leaving at least 8 feet above the ground to allow for comfortable headroom.

In unstable soils, posts will need concrete anchors like those used to set fence posts solidly (*page 66*). Posts can also be anchored to the surface of a concrete floor if metal post anchors are set in the concrete when it is poured. When the posts are in place, attach the beams across their tops with T braces or metal post supports designed for this purpose, then nail the rafters on edge across the tops of the beams. The rafters should also be nailed or attached with metal joist hangers to a ledger board that has been screwed or bolted flat against the side of the house.

OPEN GRIDS ABOVE   Many gardeners like the light and airy feeling of this basic framework and leave it unroofed, getting some shade and maximum ventilation. A popular variation, called an eggcrate grid, is constructed by nailing short pieces of lumber between the rafters. The deeper the boards in this grid and the closer their spacing, the more shade such an eggcrate pattern will give. However, it will not provide much shade when the sun is directly overhead, at the hottest time of the day, and you may want to add a man-made cover or cultivate a natural one of vines.

Almost any open rafter or grid structure makes a fine arbor for climbing plants. Once the vines are established, they provide sun-dappled shade and rustle in each passing breeze. Overhead foliage acts as a natural air conditioner, absorbing heat and giving off moisture to the air nearby.

A CHOICE OF ARBOR VINES   Flowering vines such as jasmine and honeysuckle are particularly popular as arbor plants because of their sweet perfume, but do not overlook the possibility of planting fruit-bearing vines, which offer sustenance as well as shade. One West Virginia gardener uses the grape arbor outside her kitchen as a shady retreat when the kitchen gets uncomfortably hot, and according to neighbors, the fruit from the vines is the source of some of the finest grape conserves in the Greenbrier Valley.

It is possible to choose vines that will produce a specific kind of shade. Clematis, with its finely divided leaves, provides bright, lacy shade; bushy, solidly leaved English ivy casts a denser shadow. Evergreen species give shade the year around, but in northerly areas, where the sun is especially welcome in winter, many gardeners choose a deciduous variety of vine like wisteria or Virginia

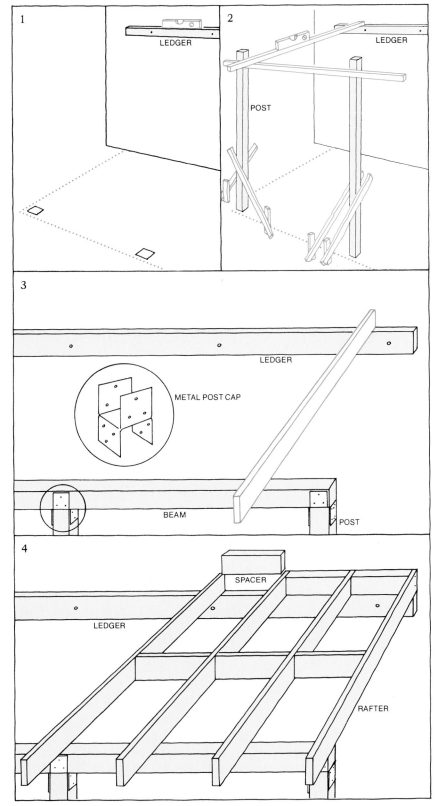

SHADY TERRACE TOPPING

1. *To build a lightweight overhead arbor to shade a terrace, first dig postholes and fasten a ledger board to the house. Lay out the desired dimensions on the ground, using the 3-4-5 method (page 58) to square the corners. Position the ledger with the aid of a carpenter's level. Attach it to the studs of the house wall with galvanized lag screws or bolts. Dig the postholes, position the posts, then anchor them in place with gravel, soil and a collar of concrete (page 66).*

2. *To trim the top of a post so it will support a beam even with the top of the ledger, use a carpenter's level to align a 2-by-4 between the ledger and the post; use the bottom of the 2-by-4 as a guide to position the beam that will span the posts. Pencil a cutting line below the beam. Before sawing the posts, brace them with scrap lumber and make sure that the concrete collars have hardened.*

3. *Span the posts with a beam running parallel with the house; it will support the outer ends of the rafters. Use metal post caps (inset) to secure the beam, nailing the downturned flaps to the posts and the upturned flaps to the beam. The chart on page 150 lists safe beam and rafter sizes for various spacings.*

4. *Toenail rafters to the ledger board and beam, then use shorter lengths of lumber as cross braces to hold the rafters in place. Additional rows of crosspieces can be used to stabilize rafters more than 8 feet long. This is desirable if further shade roofing is to be added (page 75) or to make the structure into an eggcrate grid to provide more shade.*

creeper so the leaves will drop in the fall and let the warming rays of the sun stream through.

If you need more permanent, year-round shade than that provided by an open or vine-covered framework, you can superimpose narrow boards atop the rafters, spacing them so they will give a pattern of alternating shadow and light. Structures covered in this way are called lath houses, named by some long-ago gardener who discovered that laths, the thin wood strips that were used in plastering walls, could be nailed up in a crosshatched pattern to give plants, and the people working with them, protection from the blistering rays of the sun.

Lath strips are about $\frac{3}{8}$ inch thick and $1\frac{1}{2}$ inches wide and are sold in 4-, 6- and 8-foot lengths. They need to be soaked in wood preservative unless you buy more expensive, naturally rot-resistant lath made of redwood or cedar.

TESTING SHADE PATTERNS
Before you cover a structure with lath, put up several small trial sections, leaving spaces of various widths. Nail the lath strips lightly in position. After a couple of days of observation, you will be able to pick the pattern and spacing that pleases you most. When you have decided on an optimum spacing, cut a spacer board of that width, using it as a guide to line up the laths as you nail each strip permanently in place.

As a labor-saving alternative to laths, some gardeners use inexpensive snow fencing, which is made up of lath-sized pickets held 1 to 2 inches apart by wire strands. Snow fencing is sold in building-supply stores in rolls of 50 or 100 feet and is available in such colors as green, white, red and redwood stain. Other widely used lath-house materials are battens (strips $\frac{1}{4}$ inch to $\frac{1}{2}$ inch thick and generally 1 to 3 inches wide), grape stakes (2-by-2-inch strips), furring strips ($\frac{3}{4}$ to 1 inch thick and 2, 3 or 4 inches wide) and larger boards such as 2-by-3s, 3-by-3s or 2-by-4s.

One of the easiest ways to build a lath-house shelter for a terrace is by fabricating modular units in advance. During the winter or periods of bad weather you can build lath-roofing squares in your workshop, nailing lath strips to individual wood frames. When spring comes, you can build a framework of posts, beams and rafters over your terrace, then rest the lath-covered frames on top of supporting strips nailed to the sides of the rafters. With this setup, you can move the modular units around to get any pattern of sun and shade you want, and after the hot-weather season the lath panels can be removed and stored away for the winter.

Another way to gain precise sun control without sacrificing air circulation is to slant closely spaced roof boards over a terrace so that they act as louvers. For example, if you set boards 4 to 8 inches wide on a north-south axis and angle them upward toward the east, they will admit welcome morning sun but give increasing shade in hot afternoons *(page 78)*.

There are several materials lighter in weight than laths or boards that are suitable for shading terraces. Woven reed, sold in rolls at shade shops, casts a fine, filmy shadow pattern, is easily stapled in place and is inexpensive enough to be replaced every few years. Woven bamboo and split bamboo, which are made primarily for interior window blinds, are also widely used outdoors to provide a fine, filtered shade.

When protection from rain as well as sun is needed, canvas is a very popular roof material. It can be either nailed to a wood frame or lashed to lightweight pipes anchored in concrete. Canvas, which is made of closely woven cotton, has been used for centuries to make tents, tarpaulins and garden pavilions. The most durable modern canvas, vinyl-coated duck, may last 10 or 15 years in a garden if it is given good care. To prevent mildew, always let a canvas awning dry thoroughly after a rain before folding it. The main drawback to canvas is that its dense weave blocks air as well as water, permitting uncomfortable heat to build up beneath it. If possible, leave a gap of a few inches between a sloping awning and the house wall to let

RAIN-AND-SUN SHELTER

QUICK COVERS FOR COOLER ARBORS

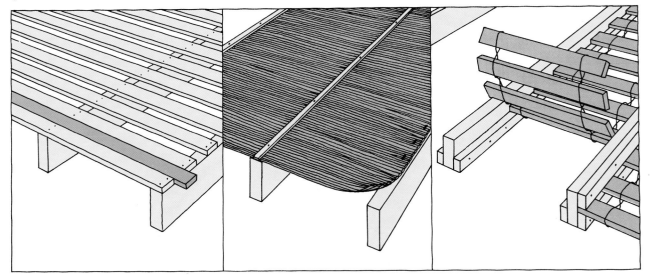

To add a lightweight roof to an overhead structure, nail wooden laths across the top of the rafters. Use a scrap board (red) to space the laths at uniform intervals, depending on the amount of shade desired.

For a roof of matchstick bamboo or woven reed, cut the material to align its edges with the rafters, then staple it on. Furring strips on top, nailed to each rafter, will prevent wind from lifting the roof.

To roof with snow fencing, rest it on inch-square wooden cleats nailed to the sides of the rafters. Cut the fencing to fit before mounting. Secure it by placing other cleats on top and nailing them to the rafters.

warm air escape. Some opaque awnings cast such deep shade that few kinds of plants can survive beneath them.

Many gardeners are taking a cue from nurseries and using shade cloth made of woven plastic, which lets in a lovely, filtered light much like that admitted by woven reed. Shade cloth is easy to handle and light in weight, and it can be stretched taut and tacked to a roof structure. One California gardener covered an entire deck with panels of shade cloth, providing just the right amount of filtered light for his scores of ferns and begonias *(page 82)*. Small-mesh insect screening provides the lightest shade of all; it is useful only where minimal sun protection is sought. It can also, of course, be incorporated into a framework to convert an open terrace structure into a bug-proof screened porch.

PLASTIC-PANEL ROOFING
Overhead panels of translucent fiberglass plastic are a practical and attractive way to shield a terrace from rain as well as sun. They let in a soft, diffused light, are available in many colors, patterns and sizes, and can be bought in kits complete with caulking compound, fasteners and filler strips. Plastic panels are sold in 26- to 40-inch widths in flat, corrugated and square-ribbed profiles. Because clear or lightly tinted plastic panels transmit nearly 90 percent of available light, they have gained popularity in greenhouse construction. The more opaque panels, which may allow as little as 20 per cent of sunlight to pass through, are generally used to reduce the intensity of strong summer sun.

Plastic panels, which can be cut to size with a fine-toothed hand saw, are commonly nailed or screwed to the tops of rafters spaced to accommodate them (2 feet apart for standard 26-inch ribbed or corrugated panels overlapped one rib). For drainage, slant the panels away from the house at a pitch of 1 inch per foot (3 inches per foot in areas that get heavy snow). As with canvas awnings, a narrow ventilation gap should be left between the panels and the house wall to avoid heat build-up.

Ribbed and corrugated plastic panels have great strength; a panel that weighs 5 to 8 ounces per square foot will support 100 pounds per square foot, far more than building codes require. If you object to the corrugated look, which reminds some people of World War II Quonset huts, you can mask the edge with a trim board attached to the framework at a right angle to the plastic, leaving a slight gap between board and plastic to allow for drainage. Flat plastic panels can also be used as roofing. In addition, they can serve as skylights in a solid roof or as rain shields over seating areas in a planted terrace that is otherwise left open to the sky.

Most of the construction techniques and materials used for

overhead structures attached to the house can be adapted for building detached arbors, gazebos, storage sheds and work centers. An arbor, an open framework with plants climbing over it, forms a cool, leafy tunnel. Arbors can be as practical as they are romantic. One gardener whose garden is very small makes every inch count; his rose arbor conceals a compost bin and storage area. "You can't see the garbage for the flowers," he explains. (Vertical latticework that does not extend overhead is called a trellis; an open overhead structure that is built of heavy rafters and beams is called a pergola.)

A garden shelter that is newly popular after many years of neglect is the gazebo, a roofed, freestanding structure that can range from the simple open platform covered with a canopy to an enclosed playhouse or poolside cabana with facilities for serving meals.

The gazebo is descended from the viewing pavilions of ancient China. Its Western beginnings can be traced to the great walled estates of 16th Century Europe, which were equipped with watchtowers where sentries were regularly posted and the ladies of the manor could safely tarry to contemplate the countryside. Gradually, ground-level versions of these watchtowers began to appear in elaborate gardens as little roofed summerhouses. They eventually became known as gazebos, a combination, some say, of the English "gaze" with the Latin *bo,* meaning "I shall." Others hold that the word is a corruption of "gaze about."

Whatever the name's origin, gazebos reached their height of fashion in Victorian times. Round, square, hexagonal or octagonal, capped by peaked or onion-shaped roofs, festooned with ornate latticework or wrought-iron filigrees, Victorian gazebos were genteel retreats where proper ladies and gentlemen could savor the wonders of nature as they sipped their tea. Larger versions became focal points in public squares and parks as sitting pavilions, politicians' platforms and bandstands.

The gazebo's return to favor may be partly nostalgic, but many gardeners also realize that a gazebo is a practical way to provide shade where none exists naturally. Because it is usually situated at some distance from the house, a gazebo can take off on any architectural tangent, from a Victorian bird cage to an Oriental teahouse to a space-age geodesic dome.

Less romantic but also very practical are structures that are designed to make gardening easier and more enjoyable. Even the gardener who has a good-sized carport or garage finds that it has its limits as a catchall for lawn mower, rakes and shovels, bags of fertilizer, garbage cans, firewood, a potting or workbench and the like. When it becomes so crowded that there is barely room for the

THE ROMANTIC GAZEBO

MORE SPACE FOR STORAGE

SETTING SUN LOUVERS

1. *When you install permanently fixed louvers on a north-south axis between the rafters of an overhead structure, slant the louvers upward toward the east so their width allows morning sunlight to penetrate but blocks out the hot afternoon glare. If you want shade in the morning and sunlight during the afternoon, reverse the slant of the louvers. Desirable winter sunlight reaches under such shade structures to bring welcome warmth to the terrace.*

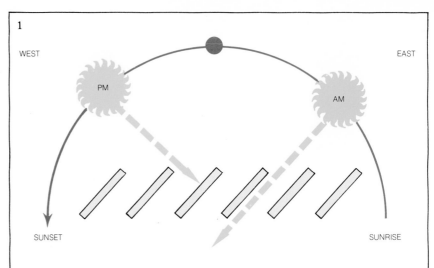

2. *If your louvers run east to west, you probably will want to slant them upward toward the north so their width deflects the hot sun's rays at midday. Early morning and late afternoon sunlight passes under the edge of the overhead to reach the terrace. However, if you slant the louvers toward the south, the midday sun will also penetrate to some extent. If your terrace does not sit squarely on the compass points, plot its location on paper and sketch in the summer sun's path overhead; experiment with your diagram until you have determined the best angle for your louvers.*

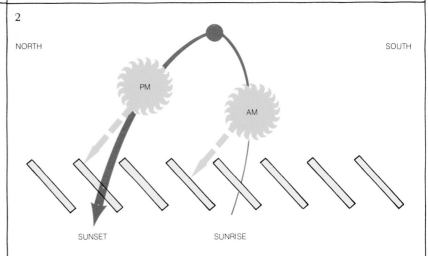

3. *When you have selected an angle for your louvers, cut wooden spacers to brace the louvers in the correct positions between the rafters. Nail the first pair of spacers to the rafters. Position a louver against them and toenail it to the rafters, then add the next two spacers. All spacers except those abutting the ledger board on the side of the house will be identical and may be cut from one board. Most louvers are 4 to 6 inches wide and are set up to 4 inches apart; narrower louvers must be positioned closer together to give adequate shade.*

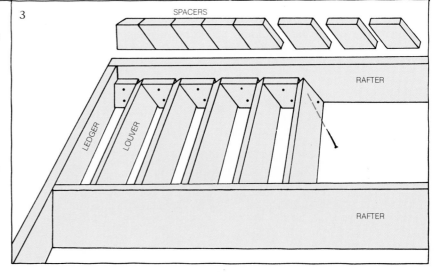

family car, it may be time to consider a storage structure designed to fit specific gardening needs.

The simplest utility structure, an enclosure large enough to hide a garbage can and a compost heap, can be built of 2-by-4s and plywood. One Philadelphia gardener has a durable compost bin built of unmortared decorative concrete blocks. The structure also houses firewood and a garbage can.

You can sometimes economize and conceal a storage or utility structure by building it against an existing house wall or a fence. In the latter case, if the hinged doors across the front of the enclosure are of the same board pattern, the structure will appear to be a natural jog in the fence.

By building a higher, wider shed and adding a workbench, you can convert a storage area into a work space suitable for repotting plants, rooting cuttings, starting seedlings and many other gardening chores. The work surface should be as long as possible, at least 4 feet long and 2 feet wide, and if it is positioned at a comfortable work height you can use it easily while either standing or sitting on a tall stool. You can build a workbench on its own legs, as a freestanding unit, or hang a sturdy shelf braced with diagonal 2-by-4s from the frame of the structure.

Make the top of your workbench of boards butted tightly together so that spilled soil and small objects like nails and screws do not fall through the cracks. The space underneath the bench can be organized to provide storage facilities for bulky items: shelves to hold stacks of empty flowerpots and gardener's flats, containers for frequently used potting materials like topsoil, peat moss, leaf mold and sand (you can build roll-out boxes or tilt-out bins for these, or you can simply use ordinary galvanized-steel garbage cans). Install some shelves above the work surface to hold smaller cans, bottles and gardener's tools; these shelves can also serve as convenient display racks for shade-loving potted plants that must be sheltered from direct sunlight. Add one or two lock-up drawers or cupboards for small items and for toxic substances like garden chemicals and wood preservatives that you want to keep out of children's reach. You may also want to have a durable, quick-draining floor of crushed rock or bricks laid in sand, and a hose connection with a sink for watering flowers and washing pots.

Whatever kind of work-storage area you decide to build, you can design it so that it can be closed during off-seasons against rain or winter snow. Or you can leave it open to the breeze year round, roofing it appropriately to provide just the amount of shade and shelter that you and your favorite plants require.

A GARDEN WORK CENTER

Man-made shade for plants or people

"Pay no worship to the garish sun," advised William Shakespeare in *Romeo and Juliet,* and shade-loving gardeners everywhere have taken this advice to heart by building shelters that screen or shut out the sun's rays. Often these overhead structures are no more than simple frameworks of wooden posts and crosspieces. Others are elaborate, solid-roofed pavilions that offer not only shade but protection from wind and rain. The choice among the many options depends on both garden and gardener: the light and heat requirements of the plants you intend to grow must match your own needs for shade and comfort. Keep in mind that the basic design of the structure, as well as the exact type of materials you use, should complement the surrounding garden and the home.

If the plants to be grown are your major concern, you will first have to consider carefully the effect of an overhead on the climate below. Many plants have quite specific preferences when it comes to outdoor living, and a minor shift in sunlight, temperature or humidity can mean success or disaster for their cultivation. Some of the most finicky plants are the species that originated in woodland or jungle; they require varying amounts of shade and may even have a special susceptibility to sunburn. For these types of plants you may wish to employ a variable covering such as shutters or shade cloth that can be changed or removed according to weather and season. With the addition of screens or walls to control wind, the garden shelter functions almost as a greenhouse in which plants that would not normally thrive in your climate can be grown with ease.

But plants are not the only beneficiaries of shade and shelter from the elements. Many gardeners design their outdoor roofing with human activities in mind—everything from sitting and reclining to formal dining and entertaining—so that family and guests can enjoy a setting filled with close views of foliage and blooms. Some people even reverse the scheme of bringing the garden into the shelter, and instead place the shelter in the middle of the garden to provide a scenic panorama without foregoing the comfort of shade.

An open grid of fir boards set on edge softens strong California sunlight for such plants as a burro's tail and other succulents hung above a bed of impatiens.

Greenhouses without glass

By filtering light and, if desired, trapping heat and moisture, garden roofs and pavilions create a protected environment for plants that may be unaccustomed to the climate in your area. For example, the greenhouse-like shelter shown below and opposite, an open redwood framework covered with woven green plastic shade cloth, allows a San Diego gardener to grow tropical jungle plants.

An angled walk of weather-resistant redwood boards set on a ground cover of crushed red lava rock leads through a garden to a sheltered area filled with tropical plants. The entrance is highlighted by the spiky fronds of two phoenix palms.

The porous shade cloth allows sunlight and welcome rain to filter through for the benefit of a staghorn fern (foreground), other ferns and begonias in conveniently raised beds. Plants in need of extra high humidity are kept in a terrarium.

An interesting interplay of light and shadow is created inside a small lath house by spaced redwood slats that temper bright sunlight

and strong wind for begonias and columneas. The overhead frame supports hanging baskets.

Verdant views from the shade

Roofed areas provide not only a haven for certain plants, but a refuge from heat and glare where you and your friends can retire to sit and admire the fruits of your labor. Whether a solidly roofed gazebo or an arbor largely open to the sky, an overhead structure creates a feeling of privacy and comfort within the garden. Wind whistling through latticework may add a pleasing melody.

A roof of crisscrossed wood strips painted white gives this terrace a classically old-fashioned look. The tight lattice provides welcome shade but not so much that figs, camellias and several types of trees cannot thrive beneath. The roof is supported by a framework of 2-by-6s.

An open eggcrate structure of redwood boards roofs the lush plant display of a Houston terrace. The plants get abundant sunlight during the day, but toward evening the boards block the low-angle rays of the sun. Shade will increase as the evergreen jasmine covers the grid.

The focal point of this garden is a
rustic, freestanding gazebo open to
views on all sides but sheltered from
rain as well as sun by a shingled roof. A
path of limestone slabs leads from
the house past a Celtic baptismal font,
now a handsome garden sculpture.

Finishing touches with a flourish 5

Few sights are as compelling as a dramatically lit garden, the trees, shrubs and flowers awash with the glow from artfully concealed fixtures. Some gardeners illuminate plants just to enjoy the theatrical effects, while others use light to extend the number of hours during which they can continue gardening or outdoor entertaining. Lighting is but one of several finishing touches you can add to your garden to make it more usable, more attractive or more fun. Beyond such basics as putting down steps and paths or building a fence or shelter, you can also make garden furniture, add a cooling pool or fountain and devise plant containers that are as attractive as those that are commercially available, but that cost far less.

A building-supply yard is a good source of inexpensive containers. Hollow concrete blocks, for example, make serviceable containers for small plants. Simply fill the holes in the block with potting mix and plant some colorful flowers that will bush out or spill down the sides. If you object to the bare look of a gray concrete block, paint it with exterior masonry paint. Some special blocks have darker hues or decorative pebbles cast in the surface.

You can use various kinds of pipe sections as planters, including the terra-cotta tiles used to line chimney flues and the larger terra-cotta or cast concrete sections made for storm drains, sewers and water mains. Sections range from 6 inches to more than 2 feet in diameter and from 1 foot up in length.

Set on end, sections of pipe can be grouped for massed plant displays; using various lengths will produce a stepped effect. Larger pipe sections, including those with flared ends, make good individual plant urns. Large pipe sections are heavy, however, and once they are filled with soil they are difficult to move.

To avoid drainage problems with a bottomless pipe section, place it on a bed of gravel, bricks laid in sand or spaced wood decking, or fill the lower third of the pipe with gravel.

A scaled-down scene of lush semitropical splendor is completed by a man-made waterfall flowing into a pond used to grow water hyacinths. The waterfall's actual size is indicated by the azaleas on the right bank.

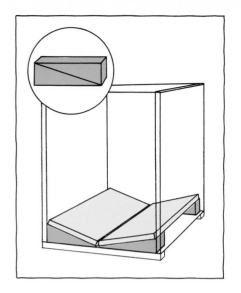

*A wooden outdoor planter that will
drain quickly and evenly after a heavy
downpour can be built by gluing and
nailing a pair of bottom boards to
wedge-shaped blocks cut from scrap
lumber (inset) so a shallow V shape is
formed. Excess water will run down
the boards and out of the planter
through the ¼-inch slot between the
boards. (A piece of mesh screening will
prevent soil from running out with
the water.) To provide roots with good
ventilation and drainage, raise the
bottom of the planter off the ground by
nailing 1-by-1-inch cleats or runners
along the bottom edges, as shown.*

Some garden centers sell old whiskey barrels and wine kegs. A
52-gallon oak whiskey barrel sawed in half will hold a large flowering shrub or small tree. (The lingering aroma can make working with
an old barrel a heady experience and possibly dangerous as well,
since concentrated fumes can be explosive; leave the barrel in the
sun and air until the fumes dissipate.) If hoops are loose or there are
gaps between the staves, fill the barrel with water for a day or two so
the wood will swell and tighten, then fill it with soil.

BOXES TO HOLD PLANTS

Rather than relying on ready-made containers, you can build
plant boxes and tubs, shaping them to your own needs. Containers of
wood are the easiest to make and are suitable for any patio or
terrace. Wood has a high insulating value and tends to keep soil and
plant roots cool and moist, even on a hot city balcony exposed to
drying winds. Frequent watering makes wood used in planters prone
to rot and insect attack but you can minimize these problems by
using a naturally resistant wood like redwood or wood that has been
treated with a preservative not toxic to plants (page 15).

Wooden plant containers can be as fancy as your carpentry
skills permit. The simplest to build is a bottomless box, used to
conceal less attractive containers or to unify a potpourri of pots.
Make several such collars of boards 1 inch thick and 4, 6 or 8 inches
high, depending on the size of the containers to be hidden. Nail the
pieces together at the corners, or join them with angle irons for
greater rigidity. Stain or paint the frames and they are ready to use.

To convert such a plant collar into a planter you need only nail
on a bottom of boards or plywood. Low rectangular boxes are useful

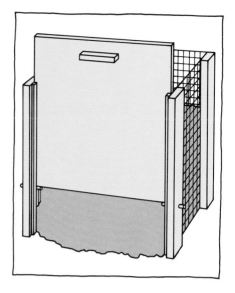

at ground level along the edge of a terrace or deck or attached to window sills or deck railings. Big, square containers will hold flowering shrubs or small trees. The larger the container, the stronger it must be. Lumber that is 1 inch thick is adequate for a small planter, but a container for a large specimen plant should be of 2-inch lumber joined with screws or lag bolts so it will not buckle under the weight of plant, soil and water.

Attractive large containers can also be made of exterior-grade plywood. To conceal the raw look of plywood edges, cover them with pieces of solid wood trim. If space is limited, attach trellises to planters so you can grow vines and such vegetables as peas, cucumbers, beans and tomatoes on them.

Any wood container will last longer if you use waterproof glue and screws to make tight, waterproof joints. Protect joints by painting them with wood preservative. To shield the entire inside of a planter, paint it with tree-healing paint or a nontoxic waterproofing compound. Use noncorroding fasteners to prevent rust streaks.

OUTLETS FOR EXCESS WATER

For drainage, it is essential that you drill ½-inch holes every 4 to 6 inches in the bottom of the container; punch holes in any plastic liner you use. If the bottom is made of several boards, space them ¼ inch apart. Cleats or casters that raise the container off the ground will improve drainage still more. You can fill a shallow container directly with potting soil if you first staple rustproof insect screening over the drainage holes to keep the soil mixes from washing through. If the container is more than a foot deep, place an inch or two of drainage gravel on the bottom before filling with soil.

It is not a big step from building planters to making other furniture for a terrace or garden. You may want to build some of the basic pieces yourself—perhaps a table and benches—that you can leave outdoors the year round; for real comfort you can buy a few well-designed chairs or lounges to sink into.

A great variety of benches and tables can be built of wood. Even a novice can easily make a bench from a single 8-foot piece of 2-by-12 redwood and a 4-foot length of 2-by-4 for a crosspiece. Simply cut two 15-inch lengths from the end of the 8-foot plank for the legs, then glue and screw them to the 4-foot crosspiece. Toenail the entire assembly to the underside of the plank and you have an attractive and serviceable bench (below).

Another easily built bench can be made of several 2-by-4s or 2-by-6s laid flat and spaced about ¼ inch apart. Nail 2-by-4 crosspieces to the undersides of the boards, then set this seat on a pair of concrete blocks placed near the ends so the crosspieces butt against the blocks. A more elegant bench calls for 2-by-4s laid on edge. Lumber has great structural strength when set on edge, and this technique is often used to make a continuous seating surface around a raised deck. If the bench is 1½ to 2 feet wide, it can substitute for a railing on a deck where the drop is less than 3 feet. On higher decks, you can build the bench into the structure of the deck but you need to attach a wide back-rest board for safety.

Low benches will suffice for informal buffet meals outdoors but if you dine frequently on your terrace or deck you may want a dining table too. An inexpensive table can be fashioned from an ordinary

BUILDING A BASIC BENCH

You can build a simple garden bench from an 8-foot length of 2-by-12 redwood (or other rot-resistant lumber) and a 4-foot length of 2-by-4. Saw two 15-inch lengths from the plank to make the legs. Glue and nail the legs to the 2-by-4, used as a crosspiece, or fasten them together with lag screws. Then toenail this assembly to the underside of the plank top and the bench is ready for use.

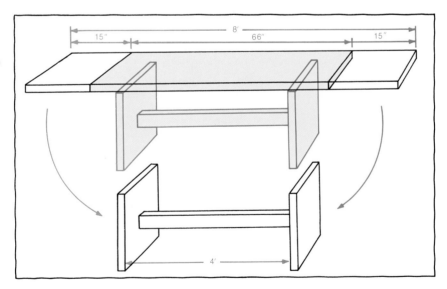

hollow-core door bought at a building-supply yard, sealed with a water-repellent stain and set on a pair of 2-by-4 sawhorses finished to match. You can make a more substantial table of redwood or cedar planks, nailing crosspieces to 6-foot planks of 2-by-6s or 2-by-8s, then resting the finished top on sawhorses or on large rectangular flue tiles set on end.

Play structures for children are as easy to put together as other garden furnishings. By planning them carefully to merge with your overall garden design, you may be able to convert them to horticultural use when your children have outgrown them. In any event, it is better to provide an equipped area for children than to nag them about playing tag in the tomato patch or Tarzan on the rose trellis.

A sandbox probably provides more pleasure for toddlers than anything else in your yard. You can build a sturdy one with four pieces of 2-by-10-inch lumber, each 4 to 6 feet long, joined at the corners with vertical wood cleats or galvanized angle irons and screws. Dig out a rectangle of sod and soil to a depth of about 3 inches and set the frame into this excavation. Shovel in a 2-inch layer of gravel to ensure good drainage, then add 5 or 6 inches of sand. Play sand is clean and white, but builder's sand costs less. A seat along the edges can be provided by nailing 2-by-6-inch boards on top of the sides. As with any play structure, bevel and sandpaper exposed edges to minimize the danger of splinters and scrapes.

If you build the sandbox of a decay-resistant wood, you can convert it into a plant bed by substituting soil for the sand. You could similarly convert any sandbox framed with weathered railroad ties, preservative-treated landscape timbers or concrete blocks.

If you have a terrace or ground-level deck floored with a grid of individual squares, you can make a pleasant sandbox simply by leaving the flooring material off one square, boxing it in and filling it with sand instead. When not in use, such a sunken sandbox, with its shovels, pails and other paraphernalia, can be concealed with a removable cover set flush with the surrounding floor. In a wooden deck, such a cover made of spaced 2-by-4s will blend in so well it will be all but invisible—and sturdy enough to walk or sit on. A cover also keeps neighborhood pets from making a mess of the sand. Filled with soil later, the inset becomes a place to display a bed of flowers or to plant a tree.

One of the unquestioned joys of summer for small children is a backyard wading pool. Plastic pools of many shapes and sizes are widely available at little cost; all you have to do is fill them with the garden hose and let the children splash to their hearts' content. But if the pool is so garish you feel obligated to empty it and put it out of

CONVERTIBLE PLAYGROUNDS

sight every evening, you might try framing it with boards, just as you would frame a sandbox. With only a little more effort, you can combine a sandbox and a wading pool into a single unit. This backyard beach can have sand and water containers separated by a low platform of 2-by-4s, with the boards spaced ¼ inch apart for drainage (below). The platform gives the children their own private sunning and sitting deck. If you like, this platform can be hinged with a place beneath for storage of pool and sandbox toys.

For many children, backyards invite climbing. If you are fortunate enough to have a strong tree with low branches, you can set a treehouse in it. A frame of 2-by-4s or 2-by-6s holding a platform of ½-inch exterior-grade plywood makes a joyful retreat. Be sure to provide a strong safety railing, with corner posts holding wire fencing to prevent falls. For the sake of the tree, drive as few nails into it as possible, since any break in the bark invites disease. Where you can, lash the frame to the tree with ¼-inch nylon rope threaded through holes drilled in the platform frame. Do not use wire; it could girdle a branch and kill it. For access, use a ladder securely attached to the frame instead of nailing climbing slats to the tree. A bed of tanbark on the ground is an added safety measure.

If your children climb on your trellises, to your dismay and the detriment of your climbing vines, build them a climbing trellis of

A BACKYARD BEACH FOR TODDLERS

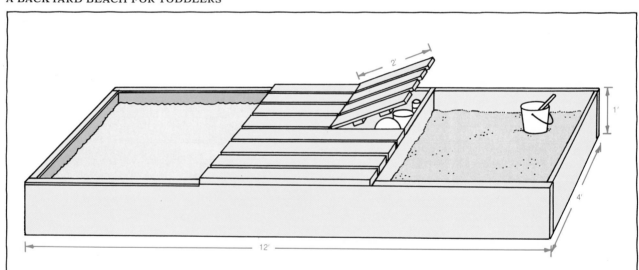

A combination sandbox-and-pool play area, designed to be converted later into a raised planter, is built within a rectangular framework of redwood. Build the frame of 4-foot and 12-foot lengths of 2-by-12s, joining them with galvanized angle irons and screws. Divide the framework into three segments with 2-by-12s nailed 4 feet from each end. In the center, make a deck of 2-by-4s, spacing them ¼ inch apart. One section can be hinged to provide a storage bin below. In the sandbox, put a 2-inch layer of gravel, then fill with play or builder's sand. Line the pool side with polyvinyl chloride (PVC) plastic stapled in place.

their own; you can convert it to plant use later. Instead of using laths, likely to give way quickly under the assault of a vigorous child, make the climbing crosspieces of 1-by-2s or dowels an inch or more in diameter. Attach these to 4-by-4-inch posts set in the ground like fence posts (page 66). Paint or stain the trellis to match other structures in your garden, and again, spread a thick layer of tanbark on the ground below to cushion tumbles.

Most gardeners, as they improve their gardens and make them more comfortable, find they want to use them after dusk for entertaining as well as for doing chores. Artificial light not only makes possible the indoor-outdoor continuity many homeowners enjoy during the day, but also eliminates the need for drawing curtains to avoid the "black mirror" look of windows at night.

Garden lighting also brings out dramatic effects often not evident during the day. For example, a clump of trees can be given a new life at night by washing the trunks and leaves with lights hidden among low plantings below. Flower colors may seem twice as vivid with the addition of one or two shaded fixtures set on short poles among the plants. Leaf patterns can be silhouetted from behind or made to cast intriguing shadows on a fence or wall.

Many a homeowner is content to mount a couple of sealed-beam floodlights under the eaves of the house, pointing them down toward the garden. This will illuminate the garden, of course, but with a harsh, flat light. A garden should be lit more like a stage set, with dominant lighting on the stars, secondary lighting for featured players and fill-in lighting for the other members of the cast. Here are guidelines to follow in planning garden lighting:

● First, make sure that any area intended to be used after dark is adequately lighted for safety. The most critical nighttime hazards are paths, steps, low walls or other changes in ground level, and garden pools or streams.

● Place some light fixtures well away from the house, perhaps even at the perimeter of the garden. They can be used to call attention to particularly attractive plants and other decorative features; they also make the garden seem larger by extending the visible space.

● Take care that the bulbs of these fixtures, and any other lights in your garden, are concealed from direct view and do not shine into your eyes—or those of your neighbor.

● To highlight a major point of interest, such as a specimen plant or a piece of statuary, and at the same time to give it a three-dimensional look, place the light source a few feet in front of and below it, slightly to one side. To keep a spotlight from making its subject appear to float disconcertingly in a sea of darkness, supply a lower level of light elsewhere, particularly in the dark middle ground between the terrace and any lighted feature toward the back of the garden. This can be done with several low-wattage lights scattered in the secondary areas, or with floodlights concealed in trees and pointing down to wash large areas with soft light.

● Consider silhouetting patterns of branches and leaves. Let the pattern appear in dark outline against a lighter background, such as a wall or fence that is washed with light from a fixture at its base. Or, silhouette in reverse, by lighting the pattern of leaves in front of a dark background; place the lights behind the pattern, aimed up so the leaves of plants become translucent.

● Interesting textures can be emphasized with grazing light. To call attention to the three-dimensional texture of a stone wall, a deeply patterned fence or a rough tree trunk, place the light source a few inches from the surface and aimed parallel to it.

● Avoid using colored lights; the results can easily become too theatrical, if not downright garish. Red light, for example, makes green foliage look a sickly brown. When in doubt, stick to white.

Before you buy outdoor lighting fixtures, walk around your garden with a portable light source, perhaps a hooded mechanic's light or a photographer's floodlight with a long extension cord. Test the light in various locations while you study the effects it gives. Then check the building-code requirements in your community; if you use standard 120-volt wiring and fixtures, you may need to hire a licensed electrician to install the lights, and the wiring may have to be sheathed in heavy conduit. But if you select a low-voltage system

LOW-VOLTAGE LIGHTING

A complete low-voltage lighting kit for garden use includes a transformer, between 100 and 150 feet of weatherproof electric cord, and about half a dozen lighting fixtures. Mount the transformer at least a foot above ground level, close by a grounded (three-hole) exterior outlet that can be switched on and off. Wherever you want to attach a light, simply make a 3-inch cut between the electric cord's two wires, remove the waterproof back of the fixture and place the split cord in parallel slots. When the back is replaced, prongs penetrate the wires to make the connection. Bury the cord 4 to 6 inches deep; some fixtures may be partially buried as well.

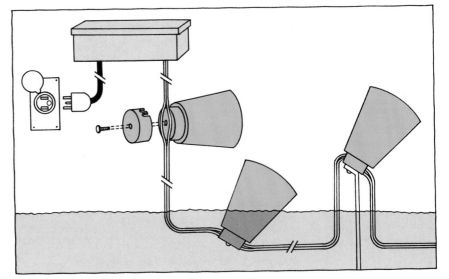

that uses a transformer to reduce house current to 12 volts, you probably need neither electrician nor permit. Such a system is economical, virtually shockproof and easy for amateurs to install. Low-voltage lighting is commonly sold in kits that contain several spike-mounted light fixtures, 100 feet or more of waterproof cord and a transformer that connects to a house outlet. The cord can simply be strung out along the ground and tucked out of sight in plant beds, while the fixtures are moved around to try various effects. Once the lights have been positioned to your liking, you can bury the waterproof cord in a shallow 4- to 6-inch trench. Remember where it is, though, so you do not accidentally cut it with a spade.

In addition to outdoor lighting, one of the most pleasant finishing touches you can add to your garden is a simple fountain or pool. Even a small birdbath adds sparkle and movement to an outdoor setting, and you can make one from any number of ordinary, inexpensive items, even the top of a plastic garbage can *(page 112)*, so long as you raise it far enough off the ground to discourage cats.

A larger garden pool need not be a complex undertaking either. Several companies manufacture rigid pool liners of formed, reinforced plastic that can be set directly in excavations in the ground. Or you can make your own pool liner, more economically, by using a flexible plastic sheeting such as polyvinyl chloride woven with nylon for added strength. PVC sheeting designed for such use is available in sizes as large as 20 by 20 feet, colored a vivid blue on one side but gray on the other in case you prefer a more neutral effect.

To make a small pool with a plastic liner *(page 100)*, first outline its shape on the ground with a piece of rope or a length of garden hose—or stakes and string for a more formal, rectangular pool—adjusting the outline until it seems right. Dig inside this outline to a depth of a foot or more, sloping the sides upward to form a rounded dish shape. Remove rocks or other sharp objects such as sticks or roots that could snag or pierce the plastic, then line the bottom of the excavation with a smooth layer of about an inch of sand. To determine the size of the liner you will need, measure the length and width of the excavation—in the case of an irregularly shaped pool the smallest rectangle that will encompass the outside dimensions—and add twice the maximum depth of the pool to each dimension. Thus a pool 5 feet wide, 7 feet long and 2 feet deep will require a liner measuring 9 by 11 feet.

Stretch the liner over the excavation, weight its edges firmly with smooth stones, concrete blocks or bricks, then start filling the center with water from a garden hose. The weight of the water will gradually mold the liner to conform to the bottom of the hole. When

A WATER-GARDEN SETTING

AN EASY GARDEN POOL

1. *To make an inexpensive garden pool without plumbing, outline it with a rope or garden hose, then excavate to a depth of a foot or more, sloping the sides toward the center. As you dig, check the depth frequently with an L-shaped jig and a carpenter's level. Remove rocks, sticks and roots, then compact the earth by bouncing and rolling a spare tire in the hole. Cut a shallow step at pool edge (inset) so you can completely conceal a plastic liner beneath the water and under a rock edging.*

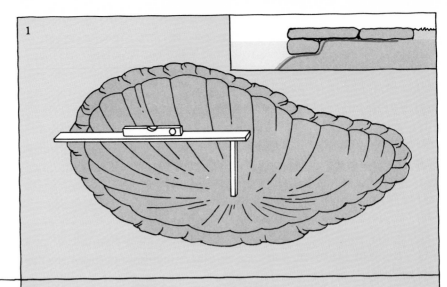

2. *Line the excavation with a durable pool liner made of polyvinyl chloride (PVC) reinforced with nylon, laid over a 1-inch layer of sand. To determine the size of the liner needed, measure the smallest rectangle that will encompass the excavation and add twice the depth of the pool plus 1½ feet for an edge lap to both length and width of the rectangle. Stretch the liner over the excavation, holding the edges in place with bricks or stones. Fill with a garden hose; the weight of the water will mold the liner to the shape of the excavation.*

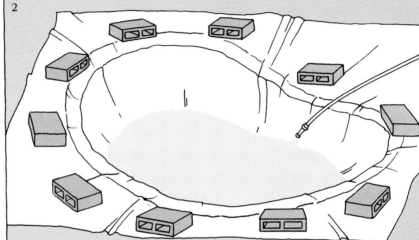

3. *When the pool is filled to within 3 inches of overflowing, trim off excess liner material, leaving a 6- to 8-inch edge flap. Hide the flap with a permanent edging of stones or, if you prefer a more formal look, use bricks or paving slabs. Add fresh water periodically to replace water that has evaporated. Drain the pool with a siphon, pump or bucket.*

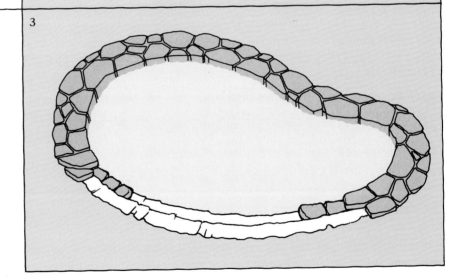

the pool is full, trim off excess liner material, leaving a flap 6 to 8 inches wide around the edge. Conceal the flap with a permanent edging—fieldstones if it is an irregular woodland pool, bricks or concrete pavers for a more formal rectangular one. You will need to add fresh water periodically to compensate for evaporation.

When you need to clean out the pool from time to time, or empty it for the winter, you can use a simple suction pump such as the kind that attaches to an ordinary electric drill. Alternatively, if you have a place in your garden lower than the pool, or a nearby basement with a floor drain, you can siphon the water out with a length of garden hose. Immerse the coiled hose in the pool. When it has filled, leave one end under the water and cover the other with your palm while carrying it to the lower position; uncover the end and the contents of the pool will be pulled out through the hose.

You can set off such a garden pool, or any of the other pools shown in the encyclopedia, with lighting, a fountain, aquatic plants, or all three. A single low-voltage bulb in a waterproof fixture will give the water gemlike luminescence at night; you can conceal the fixture below a lily pad—or buy a fixture that itself resembles a lily pad. Similarly, you can place a small self-contained submersible electric pump in the pool, propping it up with stones so the fountain tube protrudes just above the surface. Many garden centers sell such pumps, which include waterproof cords sealed into the units, plus lengths of plastic fountain tube with valves for adjusting the height and pattern of the jets; the package may also contain plastic pool liner. Most pumps operate on 120-volt current, so you will need regular weatherproof wiring and an outlet to plug the cord into.

GROWING AQUATIC PLANTS

Garden pools also offer a chance to discover the pleasures of plants that thrive in or around water. Water hyacinth, which floats on the surface, is easy to grow and a favorite for beginners. It multiplies profusely, soon filling much of a small pool with its violet-and-yellow blossoms; its dangling roots are a good spawning ground for goldfish. Waterlilies are also favorites, though they need a small container of soil at the bottom of the pool and abundant sunshine.

Once you have experimented with water-growing varieties, you may want to plant compatible species at the edge of the pool—elephant's-ear, ferns or creeping primrose, for example, or horsetail, whose tall green stems make an elegant background for a pool. You may even want to group house plants around the water during the summer, giving them the benefit of the moisture and the sun. As you sit admiring their reflections—and the other improvements you have made in the structure of your garden—you will doubtless conjure up visions of other worthwhile projects yet to come.

Painting the night with light

"Light is the first of painters," wrote poet and nature lover Ralph Waldo Emerson, and his dictum well describes the design function of night lighting for outdoor gardens: to paint a scene. By day, scene setting is carried out naturally by shifting sunlight; to paint the scene at night the gardener has a challenging opportunity to construct a display of light and shadow that will show off his work to its best advantage. But garden lighting can be more than simply a means of creating a showcase. Well-placed lighting lends safety to walkways and steps, and it turns the night garden into an extension of the house for entertaining, play or just relaxing.

To be most effective, lights should be positioned to give a feeling of balance and depth to the garden. Striking silhouettes can be created with spotlights, but care must be taken to hide the fixtures and to aim them away from the eyes of guests and neighbors. A few carefully positioned floodlights, casting a broader beam, add background light to complete the picture. Most lighting designers urge understatement; too much light imposes what might be described as an airport look on the garden. Colored lights should be handled with great discretion, for they tend to distort natural colors and give a garden a garish carnival appearance.

Before installing any permanent lights, string a network of extension cords from the house so you can try out various lighting arrangements in search of the one that works best. (Prop the cords' connecting points off the ground to guard against an accidental short circuit from moisture.) When you have decided where you want the lights, you can have an electrician install them or do the work yourself. In either event, consider employing low-voltage fixtures, which operate on relatively harmless 12-volt circuits rather than regular 120-volt household current.

For anyone who wants to dramatically extend the enjoyment of his garden, the benefits of lighting far outweigh the cost of the installation. And the possibilities of night lighting reach to the edges not merely of the garden but of the imagination.

While a floodlight gives a small garden a moonlight glow, low-voltage mushroom-shaped fixtures in a flower bed accent the end of a driveway and illuminate a path.

Brilliant by day —and after dark

With a thoughtful arrangement of floodlights, a garden that is lovely by day can be brought to life at night in quite a new and different guise. The broad beams of floods, however, may require adjustment to make the most of changing perspectives. Lights that look fine from indoors may be blinding when guests move outside. An effective way to vary the intensity is to install dimmer switches.

During the day, a terraced hillside garden stretching down to a pool appears in this naturally verdant state. The small scale of the plantings makes the garden, which is about 80 feet by 45 feet, seem much larger than it is. The depth is visually enhanced by the long, sloping walk.

Floodlit at night, the same garden reveals colors and patterns invisible by day. Since floodlights tend to flatten the illusion of depth that the gardener tried to create, three ground-level floodlights at the bases of the dwarf eucalyptus trees (top) add to their height in the night landscape.

The serenity of a still life

To capture the best aspects of your garden at night, you will probably want to highlight at least one special still-life scene—a garden sculpture, a striking plant collection or an eye-catching tree. But beware of melodrama; treat all of the garden to at least a touch of light, and make sure ground lights are positioned so they do not create a green halo effect by unnaturally irradiating foliage.

A richly textured picture is created by setting a light at the base of a guava tree so it shines up the twisted trunk and illuminates the overhanging branches. The tree is balanced by its reflection in a pool and by two mushroom-shaped fixtures that light beds and outline a terrace.

A winter-bare plum tree, its reflection caught in the blackness of a pool, becomes the centerpiece of a dramatic scene when it is illuminated by a 75-watt floodlight attached to the eaves of a house to its right. Pools radiate a tranquil beauty if lit from below with waterproof lights.

Turning things outside in

When well lighted, even a small garden immeasurably extends the living space of a house at night, bringing the natural world inside and giving a feeling of great spaciousness. But the effect is not easy to achieve.

Glass, whether in a picture window or in one with multiple panes, mirrors a lighted interior when it is not covered with a drapery. To reduce this image, the gardener must strive for a balance between interior and exterior light. He accomplishes this feat by experimenting with both lighting angles and intensities, in most cases slightly lowering interior light to reduce reflective glare. Once a balance has been established, the black-mirror look of the windows dissolves, leaving an apparently open portal into the garden.

Bright garden lights eliminate the night barrier of a floor-to-ceiling picture window, letting the garden become an intrinsic part of the house at any hour. Designed by landscape architect Thomas Church, the garden's oak-crowned elevated planting bed is illuminated by floodlights.

An encyclopedia of garden designs and materials 6

Good gardens do not simply sprout like natural forests or glades but are made from the ground up with specific tools, materials and know-how brought to bear by the individual gardener. The gardener's knowledge must include more than just care and placement of plants; to build a successful garden, it is necessary to understand construction techniques and possibilities that can provide a framework for plants to grow in and for people to sit or stroll in. The encyclopedia that follows presents in alphabetical order basic building designs and materials you will need to complete a wide variety of gardening projects.

The first section of the encyclopedia lists common garden structures, from time-tested classics like the picket fence and brick wall to artfully designed terraces and decks. Most of the designs are within the capability of any energetic do-it-yourself gardener; a few, however, may require professional help. All the designs have been chosen with an emphasis on the simple and functional, and to aid you in the choice of projects a cross-referenced guide is included at the bottom of each page.

The encyclopedia's second section lists the many types of materials available for each construction use. Since the right choice of materials is critical to the success of any construction project, the text discusses the strong points, weaknesses, relative costs and maintenance needs of the various options. Taken together, the two sections tell you not only what pattern you might use in building a deck, but what kind of wood you might choose; not only what kind of brick is available for a wall or walk, but how it can be laid.

Whether you are building a completely new garden from a sea of truck-tracked mud left after the construction of your home or merely searching for an attractive plant box, the encyclopedia offers a variety of choices compatible with diverse budgets, geographic areas, architectural styles and tastes in gardening.

The steps, walks, arbors and fences in the montage at left are among the many projects, described in the following pages, that can be made from a well-chosen selection of concrete, brick, stone or wood.

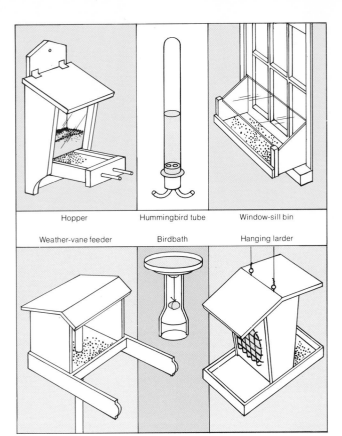

Hopper   Hummingbird tube   Window-sill bin

Weather-vane feeder   Birdbath   Hanging larder

BIRD FEEDERS AND BATHS

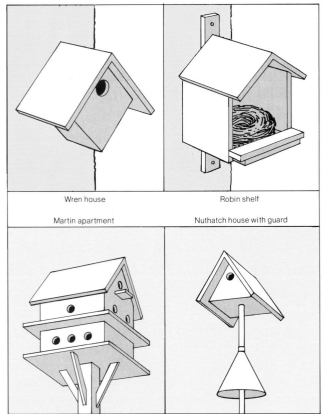

Wren house   Robin shelf

Martin apartment   Nuthatch house with guard

BIRDHOUSES

ARBORS See Overhead Structures

Bird lures

Birds are welcome helpers in any garden, devouring large quantities of insect pests as well as seeds and suet. The sight and sound of birds chirping on a feeder ledge gives a garden special charm. The type of lure you build depends on the kinds of birds you want to attract. Some species of birds like small, single dwellings while others nest in colonies. Bluebirds and wrens like a simple nesting box with a single round hole for an entrance; robins will nest on a sheltered shelf, purple martins prefer apartment complexes. The size of the entrance hole often determines the species attracted. Many other species prefer to build their own shelters. But all birds, no matter what the species, love baths.

DESIGNS

There are several kinds of bird feeders. The simplest is a platform feeder—a board mounted atop a pole and given a low rim to keep the seeds from falling off. The window shelf and tree box are variations of the platform feeder. Hopper feeders, mounted on a wall, tree or window sill, release seeds from a storage bin onto a platform below. Another type of feeder is a cage of large-mesh wire to hold suet suspended from a tree branch. Among the most elaborate feeders is the terravium, a framed glass box that is set on a window ledge and extends inside the room. Among the simplest feeders are hollowed-out gourds and coconut shells. Weather-vane feeders pivot on posts so the seeds and the birds are sheltered from the weather.

The simplest of birdhouses are boxes with open fronts or with removable or hinged tops. Roosting perches made of dowels should be placed inside; a perch outside the entrance may help enemy birds more than the occupants. Sheet-metal guards placed around the mounting tree or post, above and below the house, will keep cats and squirrels from the nest.

Although all birds like baths, they will not necessarily be attracted by all containers of water. A birdbath should be shallow with sides that slope gradually to a depth of no more than 2½ or 3 inches. Line the bottom with coarse sand or gravel; birds like a rough bottom where they can get a foothold. A simple birdbath can be made by inverting a plastic garbage-can lid atop a length of draintile; tie a weight to the handle of the lid to hold it in place.

MATERIALS

Scrap lumber, plywood, branches, wire screening and glass are common birdhouse and feeder materials. Metal should be avoided because it gets too hot. Naturally rot-resistant wood or wood that has been pressure-treated to prevent rot can be stained or left unfinished so it will weather to an unobtrusive color. Concrete and concrete-and-stone combinations are commonly used for permanent birdbaths, but high-fired clay is also suitable. Clay or concrete baths may crack if water freezes in them.

BRICK PATTERNS See Terraces and Patios, Walks, Walls

Cold frames and hotbeds

Like miniature greenhouses, cold frames and hotbeds are used for starting seedlings, cuttings or bulbs several weeks ahead of the outdoor planting season. A cold frame is heated only by the sun; a hotbed is also heated by an insulated electric cable placed under the soil. Otherwise the structures are identical. Hotbeds can be used earlier in the growing season and in colder climates.

DESIGNS
Cold frames and hotbeds are rectangular frames with transparent covers. In cold climates, both structures are set 3 to 4 inches into the ground for extra insulation. A 3-by-6-foot frame will hold four standard seed flats plus a few extra pots. A larger structure with compartments and a divided cover allows you to work in one section at a time without exposing the entire bed. The back of a cold frame or hotbed faces north and is higher than the front. The sides slope about an inch per foot so the winter sun reaches all plants and rain or melting snow will run off. A layer of sand or gravel within the frame speeds drainage. As the weather warms, the cover is propped up during the day to let excess heat escape. If a cold frame or hotbed is used only a few months of the year, it can be built with hinged sides and tops; use hinges with removable pins in the center so the structure can be disassembled for storage. In mild climates a cold frame can be mounted on legs to make it more convenient to use; in summer laths can be added to provide shade.

MATERIALS
An all-season, all-purpose cold frame or hotbed can be built with a framework of concrete blocks, bricks or a rot-resistant wood like redwood. A glass cover admits maximum light; old storm windows are often used. Glass is easily broken, however. Plastic reinforced with wire is less expensive than glass but clouds with age. A polyethylene sheet tacked to a frame of 1-by-2s makes a tough cover inexpensive enough to be replaced each year. Panels of corrugated or flat rigid plastic are long lasting but expensive.

Compost bins
Every serious gardener recognizes the value of compost, the organic fertilizer made from grass clippings, other plant refuse and animal manure. A good compost bin lets air circulate so the mixture decomposes evenly.

DESIGNS
A three-bin structure provides one space for fresh material, one for an aging mixture and one for ready-to-use compost. A single chamber with a removable centerboard that lets you convert it into a two-bin unit provides almost as much flexibility and takes up less space. Choose an out-of-the-way location where there is enough space to wheel a garden cart or wheelbarrow alongside. A bin 4 feet wide, 4 to 6 feet deep and 4 feet high will provide a supply of compost adequate for most suburban gardens.

MATERIALS
A compost bin can be built of combinations of wood and heavy-gauge wire, wood and concrete blocks, or wood slats in a wood frame. Welded-wire fencing is easy to install and allows good air circulation. Concrete blocks stacked on their sides with core holes exposed also allow ventilation; they do not need to be mortared in place. If grillwork blocks are used, such a bin can be an attractive adjunct to a garden. An unfinished wood bin, as it ages, blends well with a garden setting, but should be made of a naturally rot-resistant wood such as heartwood of cedar or redwood, or a softwood that has been pressure-treated to resist rot.

CONTAINERS See Planters

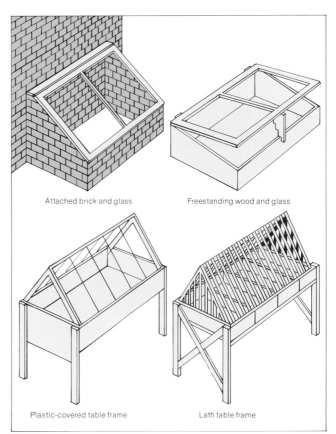

Attached brick and glass   Freestanding wood and glass

Plastic-covered table frame   Lath table frame

COLD FRAMES

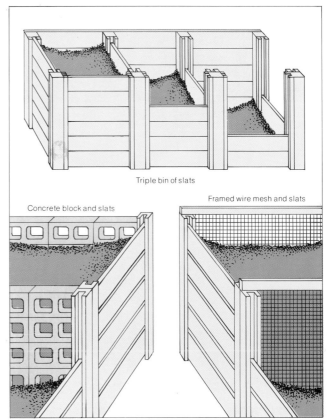

Triple bin of slats

Concrete block and slats   Framed wire mesh and slats

COMPOST BINS

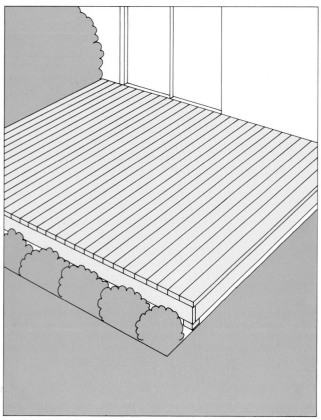

BASIC LOW DECK

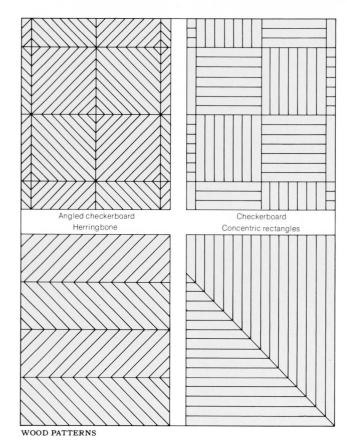

Angled checkerboard
Herringbone

Checkerboard
Concentric rectangles

WOOD PATTERNS

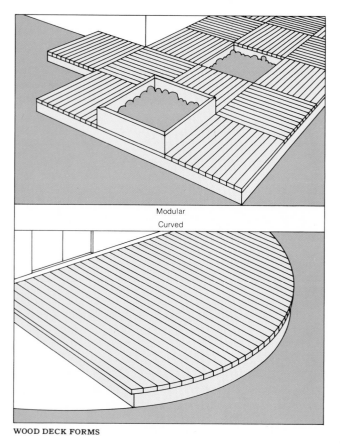

Modular
Curved

WOOD DECK FORMS

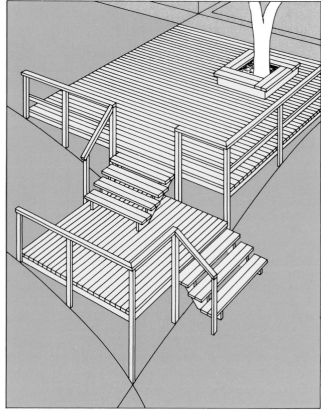

MULTILEVEL DECK

Decks

Unlike a terrace, which must be built on level ground, a deck rises over almost any terrain without grading or filling, thus converting unusable space to living space. A deck can be only a few inches off the ground or many feet.

DESIGNS

Decks sit atop carports or wrap around trees. A deck that is slightly elevated above ground level serves as an inviting transition from house to garden. A multilevel deck takes full advantage of a slope. In addition to topography, deck design must take into account local building codes, sun direction, prevailing winds, privacy and such options as overhangs, railings and built-in benches.

Building codes usually require a strong deck foundation set on sturdy footings. Such a support can be made from cinder-block piers set onto concrete footings that extend below the frost line. Decks more than 12 feet off the ground require special heavy-duty posts and crossbraces, installation work best left to a building contractor.

Once the footings and piers are in place, support posts are attached to them with anchor bolts. The joists that form the deck's outer framework are bolted to the support posts, the interior joists are attached with joist hangers, and crosspieces are nailed in place. The deck floor is nailed to this framework. Most building codes require a deck strong enough to support 50 pounds per square foot.

MATERIALS

Wood is the most popular deck flooring, although tile and concrete are also used. Dimension lumber—2-by-2s, 2-by-3s, 2-by-4s and 2-by-6s—is commonly used for decking. Lumber 2-by-8 and wider tends to cup (warp crosswise); boards thinner than 2 inches can be used for decking but require more joists to provide adequate support.

Naturally rot-resistant redwood and cedar decking can be stained or left to weather to a silvery gray. Other softwood lumber like fir and pine must be bought in pressure-treated form or soaked with a preservative.

A simple deck floor can be built of parallel 2-by-4s laid flat, spaced ¼ inch apart for drainage; the joists can be overhung 1 inch for decorative effect. A floor of 2-by-4s set on edge requires spacer boards nailed to the joists as well as twice as much lumber. Checkerboard floor is created by dividing the deck into squares and surfacing the squares in alternating patterns. This design makes it easy to leave a hole for a tree or sink a planter.

Concrete and tile also can be used for a deck surface. Concrete is relatively inexpensive but requires reinforced supports because of its weight. Tile matches concrete in durability, surpasses it in appearance and cost.

Drainage systems

Quick drainage of excess water is essential to the health of plants, even those that need abundant moisture. In places where the soil remains constantly soggy, an underground drainage system is needed to expedite removal of water.

DESIGNS AND MATERIALS

A simple system to drain waterlogged soil consists of a perforated drainpipe or loose draintiles set in a trench, covered with roofing felt and encased in 6 inches or more of coarse gravel, with the drain sloped at least 1 inch in every 15 feet. If the water problem is severe, drainage tiles may be needed to carry water to a storm drain or to more permeable soil.

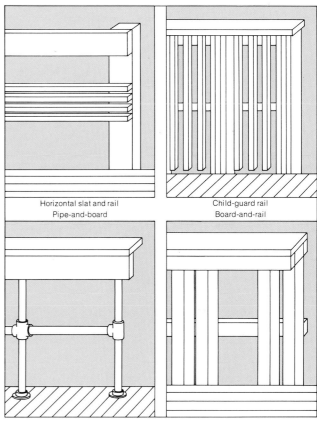

Horizontal slat and rail
Pipe-and-board

Child-guard rail
Board-and-rail

DECK RAILINGS

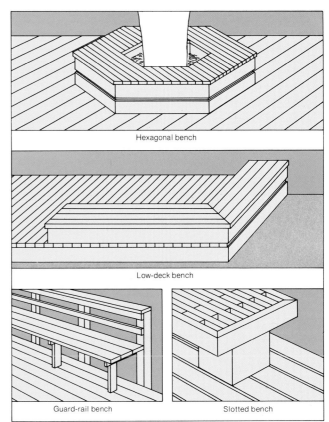

Hexagonal bench

Low-deck bench

Guard-rail bench

Slotted bench

BENCHES

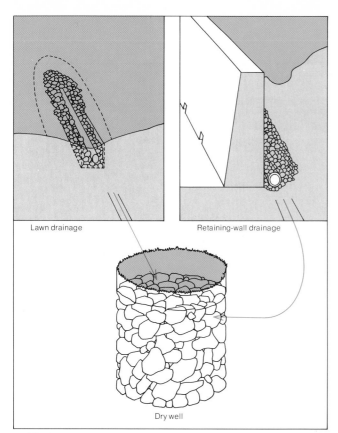

Lawn drainage

Retaining-wall drainage

Dry well

DRAINAGE

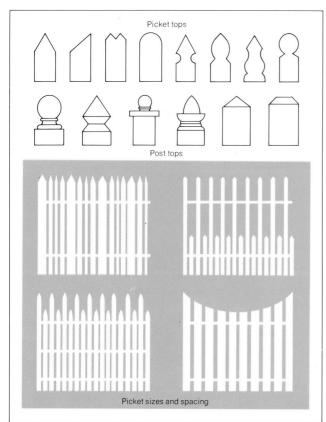

Picket tops

Post tops

Picket sizes and spacing

PICKET FENCES

In such soil, the water can be directed into a dry well, a straight-sided hole 36 to 48 inches deep filled with stones and rocks 2 to 4 inches in diameter. If the problem is slight, it may be solved with a shallow ditch filled with stones, then covered with soil. Run the ditch at a slight slope down from the wet area, taking care that the flow is directed away from your neighbor's property.

An accumulation of water behind a retaining wall is hazardous. Gravel or rock backfill will help drain that area. Weep holes—drainage holes made by inserting pipes or copper tubing at even intervals into the wall—also help keep water pressure from building up. But drainage tile behind the wall will channel water to a point where it will do no harm. A shallow surface gutter of concrete or tile in front of the wall can be used to keep water from spilling from the weep holes onto the lawn.

If you build a wooden fence in soggy ground, set the posts atop a bed of 4 to 6 inches of gravel and surround them with a 2- to 3-inch ring of gravel. Anchor them with concrete collars extending above the ground. Do not put concrete under posts; water trapped between post and concrete would rot the wood. Use caulking compound to waterproof the space between the concrete collar and the post.

DRY WELL See Drainage systems

Fences

Fences can be constructed in a seemingly endless variety of patterns for a number of purposes. They can provide privacy, serve as windbreaks or sun traps, even protect plants from the neighbor's dog or keep your own at home. A boundary fence is commonly low and open; a privacy fence is designed to block the view in and generally is at least 6 feet tall, depending on the terrain.

DESIGNS

Any fence requires a framework of posts and rails. (Some types of wire fencing come with a ready-made framework.) Steel posts usually can be driven directly into the ground. But wood posts must be set in gravel-filled holes and may need concrete collars for stability. Wood rails usually are simply nailed to the posts.

Once this basic framework is in place, the slats, boards or pickets that complete the design are attached. The picket fence, long associated with colonial architecture (pages 62-65), is made of evenly spaced, standard-sized strips such as 1-by-1s, 1-by-3s or 1-by-4s, in heights generally lower than 5 feet. Popular picket tops include triangular, rounded, sawtoothed, angle-cut, spearhead shaped and spade shaped.

The rail fence, with its low, horizontal design of rough-hewn posts and connecting rails, is used to mark boundaries where privacy is not a consideration. In a split-rail fence, the rail ends are inserted into holes in the fence posts. In a lapped-joint fence, the rails are nailed to the sides of the posts. In a mortised-joint fence, the rails fit into notches in the posts called mortises.

There are several styles of high-level fences (5 feet tall or more). A grape-stake fence is made of rough redwood boards about 2 inches square and up to 6 feet long. Originally used to hold grapevines, grape stakes can be used vertically or horizontally, nailed onto the rails like pickets or onto the posts, or fitted into a frame to make a panel. Slat fences, made of redwood or cedar in 1-by-1 or 1-by-2-inch slats, are used where a more formal look is needed.

Louver fences, with louvers running either vertically or

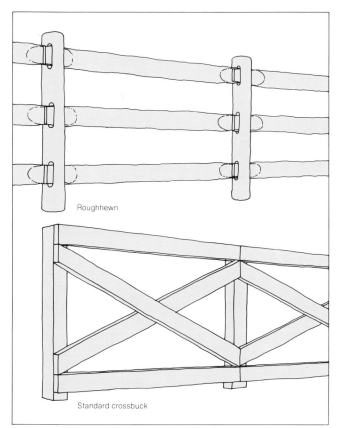

Roughhewn

Standard crossbuck

POST-AND-RAIL FENCES

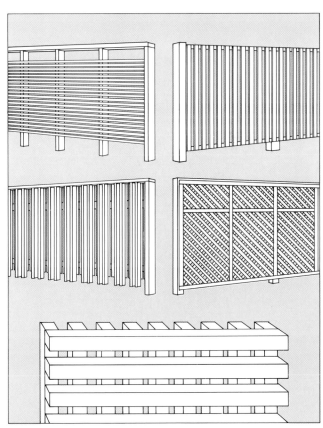

Lap joint, angled top

Posts with slats

Three-rail

POST-AND-BOARD FENCES

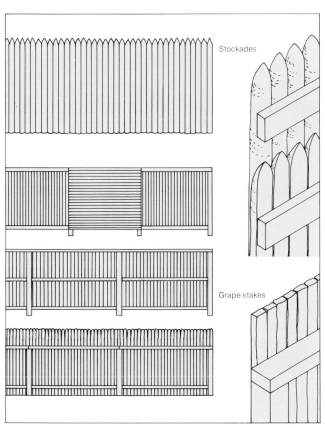

Stockades

Grape stakes

STOCKADE AND GRAPE-STAKE FENCES

LATH AND SLAT FENCES

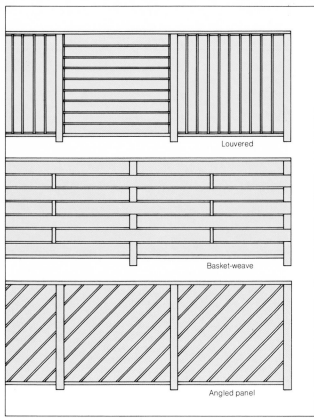

Louvered

Basket-weave

Angled panel

BOARD FENCES

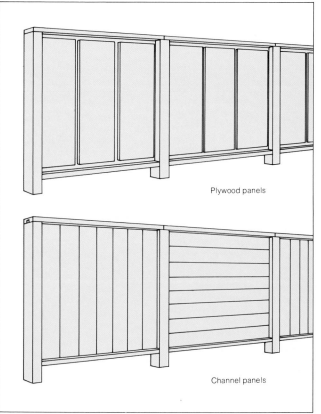

Board-and-board

Board-and-batten

BOARD FENCES

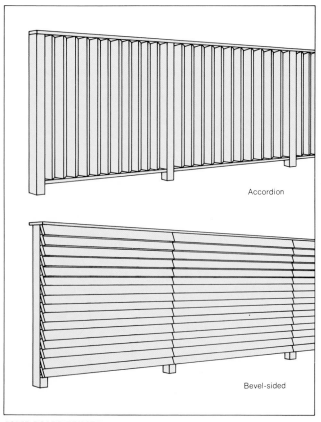

Accordion

Bevel-sided

SOLID BOARD FENCES

Plywood panels

Channel panels

FRAMED FENCES

horizontally, can be angled to control the amount of light or wind admitted to the garden. Placed horizontally, louvers give almost total privacy but they tend to warp and invite climbing. Placed vertically, louvers give passersby a chance to peek through. Louver fences require more lumber than almost any other kind of wood fence.

The solid board fence can be built with a vertical, horizontal or diagonal pattern. A vertical pattern makes a long, solid fence seem shorter. A horizontal pattern makes a short fence seem longer, stretching a small area visually. Solid board fences provide maximum privacy, but they may not stand up in areas of strong wind. A variation, the board-and-board fence, is built with alternating boards on opposite sides of the fence frame. Set vertically, a board-and-board fence is an effective windbreak. Set horizontally, it also provides privacy, but it can be easily climbed.

Basket-weave designs are attractive from either side of the fence. Prefabricated woven patterns are available in panels. Individual boards can also be woven into a fence framework. Latticework and trelliswork fences make a crisscross pattern for climbing vines, with the tightness of the spacing determining how much privacy it gives.

Solid panel fences commonly are made of exterior-grade plywood or tempered hardboard, a bonded wood fiber. A panel fence gives total privacy but the large, flat surface requires strong structural support against the wind.

MATERIALS

Wood is the most popular fencing material. Other materials that are used in home gardens include tempered glass, plastic, asbestos board, aluminum, wire and wrought iron. Panels of tempered glass, available in many patterns and colors, block the wind without obstructing the view, but they are heavy, expensive and difficult to install. Never use plain untempered clear-glass panels that someone might inadvertently walk through. Plastic panels make a practical, easy-to-handle fence and are less expensive. Plastic panels come in flat, corrugated or ribbed sheets in a wide array of colors, patterns and textures. Plastic generally looks best in combination with wood posts and rails.

Asbestos board is waterproof, fireproof and rotproof. But it is difficult to cut and its extreme weight—a 4-by-8-foot panel ¼ inch thick weighs 80 pounds—requires very strong supporting posts. Aluminum panel fencing is lighter and requires little maintenance; it comes in many designs that mimic wood fences—post-and-rails, louvers, solid panels.

Chain-link wire fencing offers maximum security. It is usually sold as a complete package including posts, rails, mesh, gates and installation. Chain-link fencing of galvanized steel or aluminum is available in heights from 3 to 9 feet and in many colors. It is also sold with a green or black plastic coating to moderate the fence's harsh look. Plastic, metal or wood strips can be laced through the links for privacy and to provide a less institutional appearance. Metal picket fences, available in rolls or strips 36 to 48 inches high, are used to border flower beds.

FOUNTAINS See Pools

Gates

While many gates serve the purely practical function of closing in small children and pets or asserting the right of privacy, gates frequently help set the mood of a garden. Low, open and inviting or tall, solid and imposing, a gate can complement the adjacent fence or contrast sharply with it.

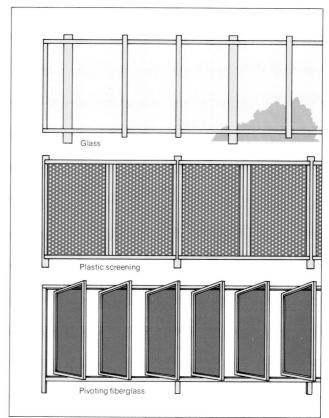

GLASS AND PLASTIC FENCES

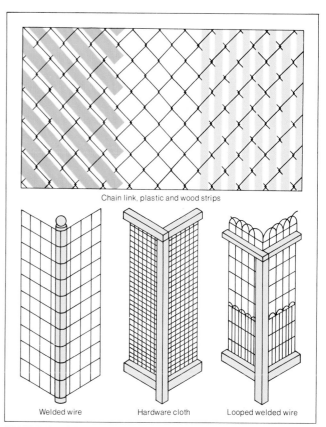

CHAIN-LINK AND WIRE FENCES

119

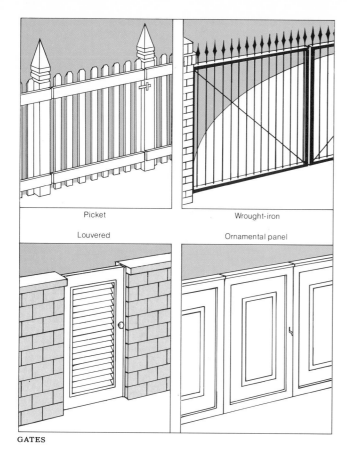

Picket
Wrought-iron
Louvered
Ornamental panel

GATES

Back lighting
Uplighting
Silhouetting
Underwater lighting

LIGHTING EFFECTS

DESIGNS

When you design a gate, consider the traffic that will flow through it and the abuse it will need to withstand. The gate's width, its weight, its latch and hinges and its posts are all important design factors. A gate should be wide enough to accommodate two people walking abreast, one person carrying a large package, or one wheeling a piece of garden equipment like a wheelbarrow or a lawn mower. But gates more than 4 feet wide often sag of their own weight if they are not firmly supported. For a wide span, consider a two-part gate that opens at the center.

Choose the latch and hinges before you start to build the gate. The weight of the latch and the way it operates must be compatible with the design of the gate and the materials of which it will be constructed. Decide in advance how much security you really need and how much stress the latch should be able to withstand.

Flimsy or poorly attached hinges are a primary cause of gate failure. Hinges can be built into masonry posts and fastened onto the adjacent gate, or they can be attached to surfaces of both post and gate. Either way, they must be strong enough to support the weight of the gate and take the abuse of frequent swinging and slamming. Squarely constructed masonry gateposts will form right angles with the gate. If the gateposts are of wood, they need to be stronger than the other fence posts. They can be set in concrete collars bolted to metal anchors set into concrete piers, or sunk at least one third of their length into the ground.

Metal gates or fittings should be primed and painted to prevent rust. To keep the gate from sagging and binding, keep hinge screws tight. Reset leaning posts, or pull a hinge post back into place with a turnbuckle and wire by running the wire from the top of the gatepost to the bottom of a nearby fence post.

MATERIALS

A gate similar in materials and design to its fence will blend in with it, while one made of contrasting materials will stand out and may seem more inviting. Wooden gateposts should be 4 by 4 inches for gates up to 5 feet high, 6 by 6 inches for taller gates. Any lumber that is used in gate construction needs protection against rot. Simple wooden latches can be made in your workshop; a wide assortment of metal latches ranging from hooks and hasps to locks with sliding bolts are available at hardware stores.

GAZEBOS See Overhead Structures

HANGING BASKETS See Planters
HOTBEDS See Cold Frames and Hotbeds

LATH HOUSE See Overhead Structures, Storage

Lighting

By illuminating trees, shrubs, plant beds, walks, steps and terraces, outdoor lights extend the enjoyment of a garden into the evening hours. When skillfully placed, they can have a dramatic effect.

DESIGNS

A well-designed lighting system places emphasis on the effects that are produced by the lights, not on the lights themselves. A variety of effects can be produced by aiming the light sources in different directions. A light placed behind a tree and aimed upward will silhouette the tree; a light that is positioned in front and aimed upward will cast a shadow pattern on a wall behind it. Downlighting can call attention to a single plant or produce a soft, diffused effect over a broad area. Downlighting is also the best for illuminating steps and walks to ensure safety.

To make the garden seem as large as possible (and to draw insects away), place some lights at the perimeter. For an area such as a terrace where bright light is only occasionally required, a waterproof dimmer switch is desirable. Waterproof submersible light fixtures are also available for use in pools and fountains.

MATERIALS

Two systems are available for garden lighting. One uses the standard 120-volt house current; the other, a low-voltage system, employs a transformer to reduce the current to only 12 volts. A high-voltage system produces brilliant light but its installation outdoors is complicated and can be hazardous. Low-voltage lighting is safe; the fixtures are small, lightweight and easily concealed in the garden; the cost of operating the system is low.

The simplest kind of low-voltage transformer plugs into any outdoor receptacle. The amount of current that a transformer emits, usually between 72 and 330 watts, determines the number of fixtures and the length of wire that can be used. Transformers of 126 watts are adequate for most gardens. This system can be turned off by pulling the plug, but it is more convenient to have the outdoor receptacle controlled by an indoor switch. Some low-voltage systems are controlled by photoelectric cells, so the lights automatically go on at dusk and off at sunrise.

The cables of both the 12-volt and 120-volt systems are buried, but your building code will probably require that 120-volt cable be sheathed in waterproof metal conduit or heavy plastic, and be buried at least 18 inches deep. The cables used for low-voltage systems need be buried only deep enough to keep them from being accidentally cut.

In either case, garden lights can be positioned anywhere you want them if you use branching cables to supply power; the objective is to have effective light sources but make the fixtures unobtrusive. If a low-voltage fixture is mounted in a tree, the cord is just stapled loosely to the trunk where it is least likely to be seen. Low-voltage fixtures set in plant beds should have an extra foot or so of wire buried next to them, so they can be moved without rearranging the whole system.

Overhead structures

Elevated shelters protect plants and people from sun, wind and rain. They can cover terraces and decks that adjoin a house or that stand alone in a garden. In such classic forms as arbors, lath houses, pergolas and gazebos they provide private and tranquil garden retreats.

DESIGNS

The arbor, a freestanding open structure of overhead and side pieces that resembles an inverted "u," supports climbing vines and shrubs with its latticework. Elaborate arbors may include pillars and intricate roofs; they are sometimes attached to houses. When the overhead lattice strips are parallel and side and end panels are added, an arbor becomes a lath house. The pergola is an open overhead structure built with heavier beams and rafters. It will support vigorous climbing plants like grapevines and wisteria and is sometimes used to lead from one part of a large garden to another.

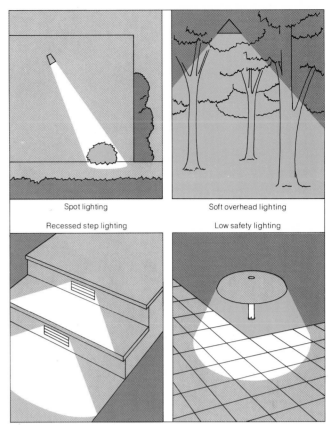

Spot lighting

Soft overhead lighting

Recessed step lighting

Low safety lighting

DOWNLIGHTING

ATTACHED ARBOR

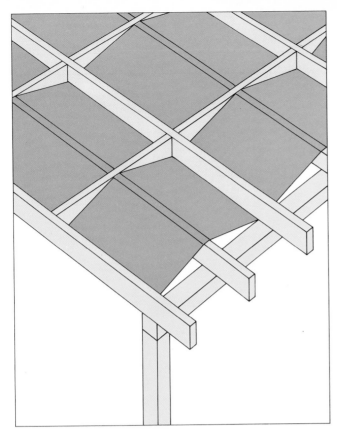

CANVAS ROOF

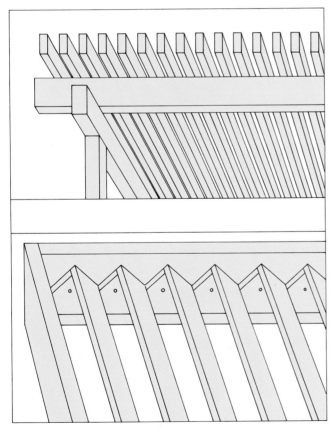

LOUVERS

The gazebo, a romantic structure often associated with the Victorian age, is a small roofed pavilion that is open on all sides, though it may be screened. It is especially useful for providing shade where there are no trees. It can be rustic, even made of roughhewn logs with a thatched roof, or it can be elegantly formal.

FRAMEWORK

Most overhead garden structures have frameworks of posts, beams and rafters. The framework for a roof that covers a terrace is attached on one side to a board called a ledger, which in turn is attached to the house; the other sides of the framework are supported by posts. A freestanding structure is supported only by posts. The weight of the roof often determines the materials used in the frame; a lace-on canvas roof can be supported by light ¾-inch pipe; a heavy wood grid requires strong 4-by-4 wood posts or steel supports.

Preservative-treated wood posts can be sunk directly in the ground where building codes and a mild climate permit. In northern areas, where frost heaving is a problem, such posts should be set in concrete for stability. Posts 11 feet long can have 8 feet above ground to give comfortable head-room and 3 feet below ground. When the posts are set, the beams are attached to them with metal T braces, then the rafters are nailed to the beams. A closed roof should slant at least ¼ inch per foot so rain and melted snow will run off. The structure must be strong enough to support your weight as you build or repair it.

ROOF MATERIALS

The overhead frame can be covered with a variety of materials, including wood, reed, bamboo, wire screening, canvas, plastic shade cloth or panels of plastic, fiberglass or aluminum. Select a covering that suits the house design, meets the shade requirements of plants below and is easily maintained.

Wood offers the widest range of roof possibilities. A simple but elegant overhead can be made from short pieces of lumber set between rafters in an open eggcrate pattern. Lath or batten strips, in crisscross patterns, will support climbing plants and increase the strength of the structure. Heavier pieces of lumber can be slanted as louvers, either fixed in place or bolted with wing nuts to make them adjustable. Treat wood structures with a preservative and be prepared to renew paint or stain every few years.

Woven reed or bamboo shades make an inexpensive cover for an overhead structure. They can be left free to be rolled up or down to provide varying amounts of shade and can be taken down for the winter. As a terrace roof, canvas blocks so much light that few plants will thrive under it. Panels of plastic, flat or corrugated, come in many shades and tints of colors that permit you to select the amount of light transmitted. Plastic can be left in place year round but tiny surface scratches will trap dirt and reduce light transmission.

PATHS See Walks
PATIOS See Terraces and Patios
PERGOLAS See Overhead Structures

Planters

Placed in front of a window, a planter seems to bring the outside in. A round planter backed by a low wall accentuates the natural curves of a garden. A hanging planter adds vertical dimension. Additionally, by raising plants off the ground, planters usually make weeding and transplanting easier and deter many garden pests.

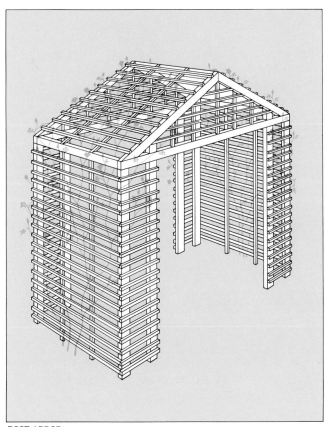

ROSE ARBOR

LATH HOUSE

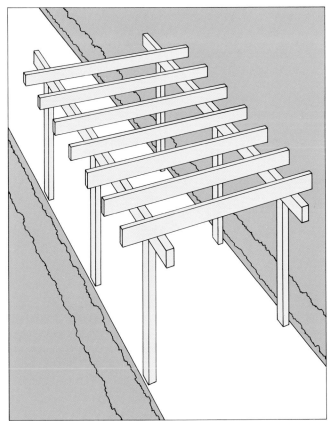

PERGOLA

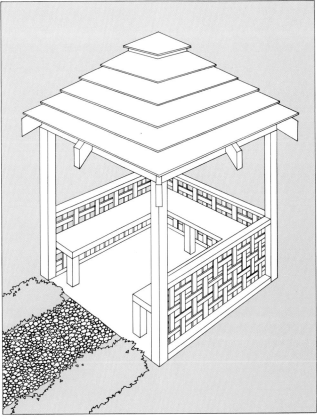

GAZEBO

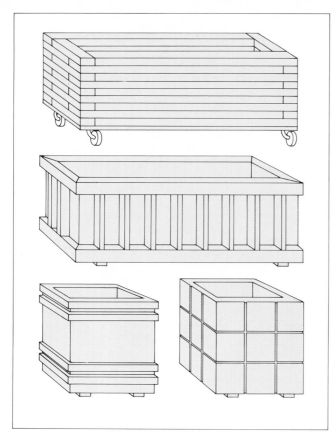

WOOD PLANTERS

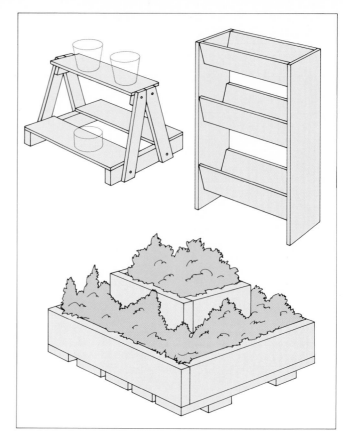

MULTILEVEL PLANTERS, DISPLAY SAWHORSE

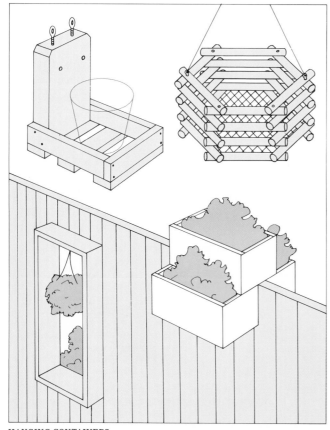

HANGING CONTAINERS

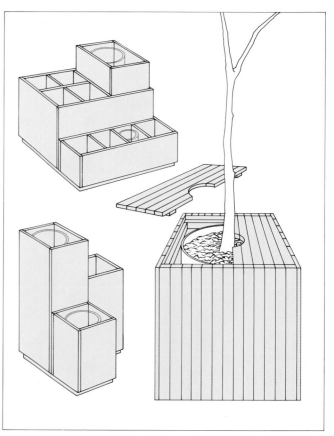

CAMOUFLAGED CONTAINERS

Bird lures, page 112;   Cold frames, 112;   Compost bins, 113;   Decks, 115;   Drainage systems, 115;   Fences, 116;   Gates, 119;   Lights, 120;   Materials, 140.

DESIGNS

When designing a planter, bear in mind how and where it will be used. A long brick planter for the edge of a terrace should be low and unobtrusive, about seat height. A wooden planter for a dwarf tree should not be so small that the tree will quickly outgrow it. As a general rule, the more elaborate a plant's foliage, the simpler its container should be. Use square and octagonal shapes for narrow trees and plants, oblong shapes for plants with horizontal spreads of foliage.

Permanent planters can be built in even, geometric shapes or with irregular curves. A window box is converted to a portable planter with a set of casters; it also can be set on the ground, mounted on wood cleats that will provide enough clearance for ventilation and drainage.

Most off-the-ground planters are suspended from wires, but they can also be built onto the top of a fence, placed on a shelf, bolted to a fence or post or set in a window that has been cut into a fence. Staging devices such as a sawhorse with shelves or raised planting troughs can also be used to gain height in a flower display.

MATERIALS

Wood and masonry are the most popular planter materials. Cedar and redwood are popular because they are naturally rot-resistant; pressure-treated timbers can be used for large-scale constructions. Fasten wood joints with galvanized nails or screws. Permanent masonry planters can be made from a variety of materials, including brick, concrete block or tile. All require poured-concrete foundations. Smaller, portable planters also can be made from materials originally intended for other uses. An oak keg or soy-bean basket will hold a large plant or small tree. Concrete drain or sewer pipes and chimney tiles are also easily adapted as planters if they are lined with wire mesh to hold in soil.

Pools

When a garden needs a focal point, it is almost impossible to go wrong with a small, imaginatively designed and well-placed pool, especially one that contains aquatic plants.

DESIGNS

Pools with clearly defined geometric shapes best suit a formal garden; those without perpendicular sides or sharply defined edges are more easily fitted into a casual setting.

A pool that is set into the ground can be protected with a 2- or 3-inch lip to keep rain water from running into it; a small spillway on one side will direct any overflow. In a pool raised above the ground, the water level can be maintained with a drainpipe or a small pump. A pool for plants or fish should be at least 18 inches deep and get at least four hours of direct sunlight daily. If there are toddlers around, a pool this deep should have a safety screen a few inches beneath the water's surface, secured to pipes, pegs or bricks.

MATERIALS

Any watertight container such as half a barrel or an old horse trough can be used to make a small pool that you fill and empty by hand. Many manufacturers offer molded plastic shells. A larger, more permanent pool can be made with concrete poured over a framework of wire mesh. If such a shell is painted a dark color, the pool will look deeper.

Nearly as permanent as concrete and much easier to build is a pool that is simply an excavation in the ground lined with a sheet of polyvinyl chloride (PVC) plastic reinforced with nylon. When the pool is filled, the weight of the water molds the plastic to the excavation; a border of rocks or bricks

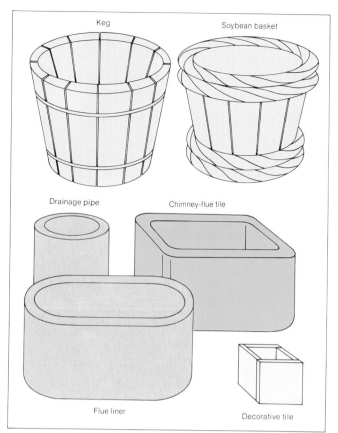

IMPROVISED PLANTERS

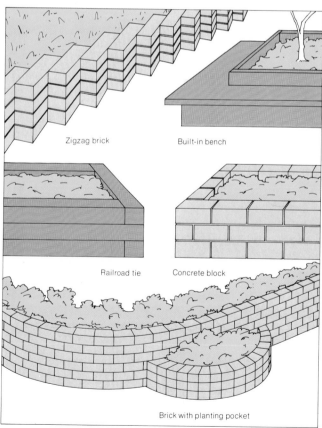

RAISED BEDS

Portable Keg

Brick pool with fountain

Plastic-lined pool

Poured concrete

POOLS

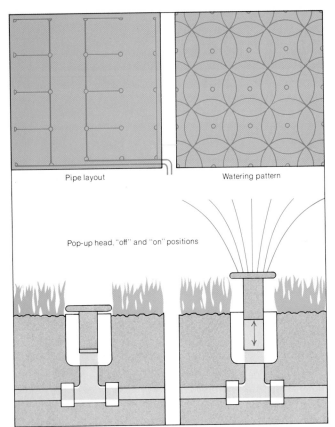

Pipe layout

Watering pattern

Pop-up head, "off" and "on" positions

UNDERGROUND SPRINKLER SYSTEM

conceals the plastic edges and holds them securely in place.

A small electric recirculating pump will turn any small pool into a fountain. A pump no larger than a softball will lift a continuous stream of water several feet into the air.

POTTING SHEDS See Storage Structures

RAILINGS See Decks
RAISED BEDS See Planters
RAMPS See Steps
RETAINING WALLS See Walls
ROOFS See Overhead Structures

SCREENS See Fences, Overhead Structures, Walls
SHADE See Overhead Structures, Fences, Walls
SHEDS See Storage Structures

Sprinkler systems

An underground sprinkler system, connected to the house water supply, can be arranged in a precise pattern so that it will spray all of a lawn evenly, freeing a gardener from hours of watering with a hose.

DESIGNS

To determine the number of sprinkler heads needed, draw a scale plan of your yard. Then place a sheet of thin paper over the plan and plot the spray pattern with a compass, overlapping the circles by a quarter of the diameter. Locate quarter-circle heads at corners and half-circle heads at edges.

MATERIALS

A system of polyvinyl chloride (PVC) pipes and plastic sprinkler heads that pop up when water is turned on can be laid out aboveground to check spray patterns before the pipes are buried. Such PVC piping is less expensive than galvanized iron, is noncorroding and carries more water than galvanized pipe of the same diameter.

PVC pipe is easy for the home handyman to install, since it is simply set in a narrow slit trench. Installing metal pipes requires the use of heavy wrenches; a wider, deeper trench must be dug to work with them comfortably. Sprinkler heads must be flush with the sod when they are off so they will not impede a lawn mower. Drain the sprinkler pipes before the first frost to prevent freezing water from bursting metal pipes or cracking PVC.

STAIRWAYS See Steps and Ramps

Steps and ramps

If you need to connect one level of a garden with another, a flight of steps or a ramp is the most obvious solution. But beyond their primary functions, they can also serve as retaining walls, or as bases for planters, or as supplemental seating space. Steps can be one of the most arresting features in a garden's design, leading the eye straight ahead, at right angles or around a gentle curve.

DESIGNS

Steep, narrow steps discourage access, while wide steps with a gentle rise seem to issue an invitation to stroll through the garden. As a general rule, the smaller the riser of a step, the wider the tread should be. For safety, outdoor steps need an absolute minimum tread width of 12 inches and a maximum riser height of 6 inches. Twice the height of an outdoor riser plus the width of the tread should equal 26 inches.

Rarely used steps can be as narrow as 2 feet, but a minimum width of 4 feet is needed to accommodate one person carrying a plant tray, and 5 feet is more comfortable if two people ascend at the same time.

When you plan steps that will rest directly on sloping ground, fit the slope to the steps. Otherwise you may create a hazardous, unequal tread-riser relationship. Cut the bank or fill under the steps as necessary to achieve a comfortable, well-designed incline.

If the change in level is slight and space is not limited, a ramp may offer an easier passage. A ramp is necessary for a wheel chair, safer than steps for the elderly or the handicapped and a convenience for any gardener moving wheeled equipment from one level to another. A ramp should have a slope no greater than 5 to 10 per cent, which means a rise of 6 to 12 inches for each 10 feet of horizontal distance. Like stairs, ramps can rise straight, turn or curve.

MATERIALS

Any material chosen for steps should be harmonious with the garden. Natural materials—wood rounds, stones or even railroad ties—give an informal appearance, while brick, concrete or clay tiles offer a formal, more structured look. If you want steps that will be inconspicuous, use materials found elsewhere in the garden; if you intend the steps to be a garden accent, use contrasting materials.

The simplest steps to build are those that use only graded soil for treads. Wood, brick or concrete risers can be held in place with stakes or pipes. The treads can be paved with gravel or wood chips, or planted with a low ground cover. If you use grass for this purpose, make sure the treads are wide enough to permit easy mowing.

Storage structures and work centers

Storage structures help to keep tools in good condition, and a well-organized work center for potting also makes gardening more fun. Although the sizes, shapes and designs of storage structures vary as much as they do in home architecture, most provide floor space for large equipment such as lawn mowers or wheelbarrows, shelves for smaller items like pots and sprayers, and a wall on which to hang small tools.

DESIGNS

Choose a convenient location for your storage structure. It might be attached to a garage with a compost bin and cold frame close by. Incorporated into a fence, or built as a long, narrow unit, a storage structure can do double duty as a screen to hide a service area or unsightly view. Built at one end of an existing terrace, a storage structure can create a sheltered corner and serve as a hideaway for barbecue equipment and patio furniture as well as garden tools. Potting areas, sometimes equipped with running water, are frequently incorporated into storage structures, though they are often built as separate units. Bins to hold bulky soil mixes and fertilizer as well as locked cabinets for the safe storage of poisonous substances can be included. Storage structures are generally small enough to merge easily into the landscape.

Before beginning construction, check your local building codes. To get a permit, you may need only a simple sketch, a list of the materials to be used and foundation plans.

The first step is to build the foundation. Excavate the area, put in a drainage layer and then the paving surface (see Walks). A finished floor of a permanent paving material such as brick or concrete should be at least 4 inches above the surrounding ground. A quick-draining floor of a loose paving

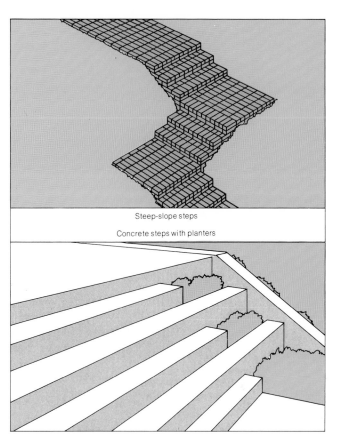

Steep-slope steps

Concrete steps with planters

BRICK AND CONCRETE STEPS

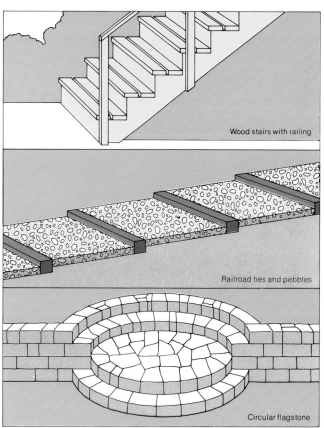

Wood stairs with railing

Railroad ties and pebbles

Circular flagstone

WOOD, AGGREGATE AND STONE STEPS

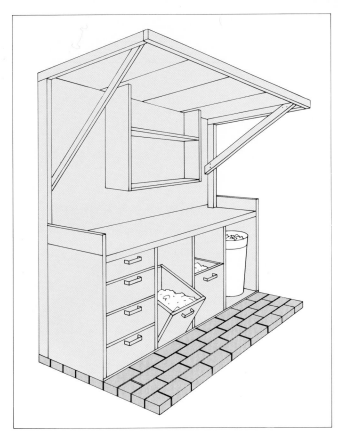

BASIC POTTING CENTER

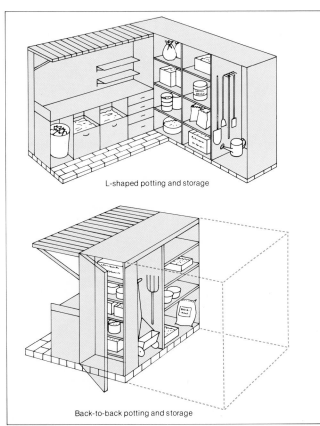

L-shaped potting and storage

Back-to-back potting and storage

WORK CENTERS

material such as gravel or wood chips should be at least 4 inches deep. Corner posts, beams and wall studs are put up next, supported by temporary braces until rafters are put into place. Most structures will use 4-by-4 posts for support; these should be set firmly in the ground, at least 6 inches below the expected frost depth *(page 143)*, and should be given concrete collars. Beams and rafters, which connect the posts and give stability to the structure, may be nailed to the posts or attached with special metal hangers. Wall coverings, applied next, are usually attached directly to posts and 2-by-4 wall studs. Roofing, with a slight pitch for drainage, follows. Finally, install shelves, hooks and bins.

MATERIALS

While storage structures and potting sheds can be built of either wood or masonry, wood construction is more common since it is less expensive and easier to handle. Redwood and cedar are popular because of their natural rot resistance; exterior plywood is used because of its versatility and the speed with which construction can be completed.

The material used to roof a storage structure depends on how it is to be used. Lath, bamboo screening or snow fencing admit light, air and rain but moderate the heat and glare of the sun. Where more security or protection is desirable, solid roofing materials are used. Those available include plywood, hardboard, asbestos board and asphalt or wood shingles. Plastic, glass or fiberglass offer protection from the weather while admitting light. Plywood, hardboard, sheet metal, asbestos board or tile are all possible materials for potting-bench surfaces, which must withstand spilled liquids. Flooring can be made of brick, concrete, gravel or bark chips.

Terraces

Whether you call it a terrace or a patio, a hard-surfaced outdoor living area increases the spaciousness of your home by providing additional room for working, dining and entertaining. Terrace designs range from a small and sheltered area outside a bedroom to a major transition space melding house and garden. A terrace broadens gardening possibilities, too, by providing a place near the house for container-grown plants and either raised or sunken planting beds.

DESIGNS

Size and site influence the design of a terrace and determine whether it is left open on all sides or is embellished with an overhead structure or shielded from view with a fence. The terrace floor can be divided into intimate spaces with islands of plants or with low walls and raised beds that double as seats. If space is limited, a small terrace can be made to appear larger by extending the flooring around a corner or by rounding the outer edges of the terrace area.

Fences or overhead structures may be useful in some locations for wind control and shade. Overheads are often needed for terraces placed to the south of a house, where they get many hours of sun. A west-facing terrace is cool in the morning but may be uncomfortably hot later in the day if not shaded. A terrace with a northern exposure is coolest, since it receives little direct sunlight. An eastern exposure may be the most desirable location of all; it is warm in the morning, cool in the afternoon and seldom needs shade.

MATERIALS

The choice of a flooring material for a terrace depends on cost and anticipated use. Loose aggregates like crushed rock and gravel are inexpensive, but they are best suited for a

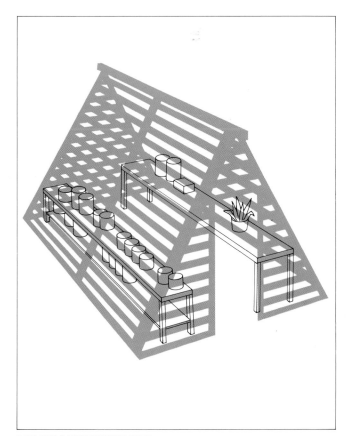

A-FRAME LATH POTTING SHED

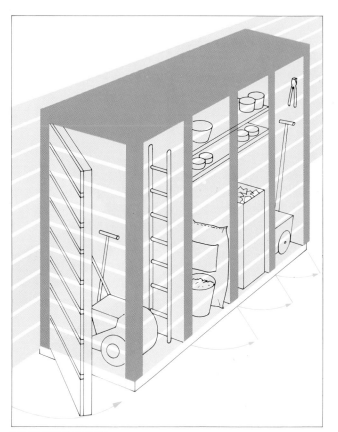

FENCE STORAGE UNIT

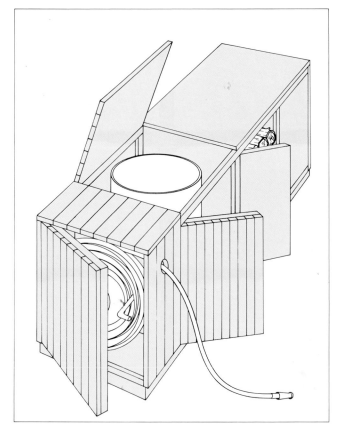

COMBINATION STORAGE UNIT

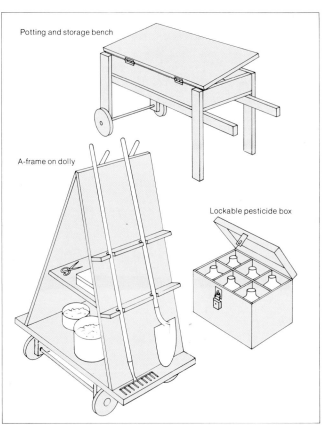

Potting and storage bench

A-frame on dolly

Lockable pesticide box

PORTABLE STORAGE UNITS

TERRACE IN HILLSIDE

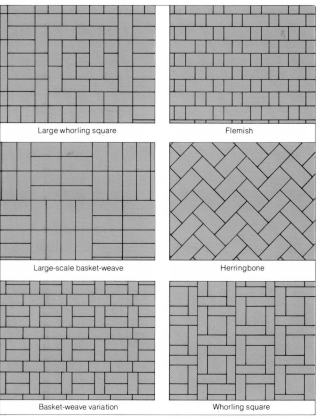

MULTILEVEL TERRACE

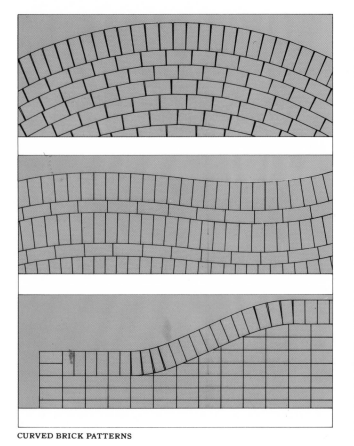

CURVED BRICK PATTERNS

BRICK PATTERNS

Large whorling square

Flemish

Large-scale basket-weave

Herringbone

Basket-weave variation

Whorling square

lightly used area where they will not need frequent grading or replenishing. A solid paving material is more durable.

Bricks provide a comfortable, nonglare terrace floor. They can be mortared to a concrete slab or set loosely in a bed of sand or soil. Because they are small and uniform, bricks seem to enlarge an area. Larger pavers such as flagstone, which may need wide mortar joints, make an area seem smaller. Flagstone is available in both regular and irregular shapes. It, too, can be placed on top of soil or sand or mortared to a slab of concrete.

A poured concrete slab is durable and, compared with brick or tile, inexpensive. But unless it is given a decorative finish, a concrete slab may look more like a parking lot than a terrace. Tile is smooth, colorful and expensive. It can be set in mortar on a concrete base or laid atop sand. Tile can create decorative insets in floors of other materials.

Wood, in squares or rounds, can be set in sand. Wood is glare-free and handsome, but even when preservative treated, it tends to warp or rot in wet locations and crack in heavy frost. Wood planks can be used to build a terrace floor if they are raised a few inches off the ground for drainage.

Adobe bricks laid on sand may crumble around the edges in moist regions if not made with an asphalt stabilizer; they are most widely used in the Southwest.

TOOL SHEDS See Storage Structures

Trellises

A vertical structure designed to support climbing plants, a trellis can also serve as a windbreak or privacy screen, support greenery that will soften a long, bare expanse of fence or wall, accent an entrance or provide an interesting background for flower borders and other plantings.

DESIGNS
Most trellises consist of crisscrossed strips of wood nailed to frames; a network of string or wire that supports a climbing plant is also considered a trellis. A trellis can be a permanent structure on posts set in the earth or a self-contained, movable unit incorporating a planter from which vines can climb and spread. When overhead latticework is added, a trellis becomes an arbor. A portable trellis can be stored for the winter, but a permanent trellis should be attractive enough to stand inspection while it is bare.

If heavy, woody vines are grown, sturdy latticework of 1-by-2s or 1-by-4s is required. A trellis of 2-by-4 crosspieces nailed to 4-by-4 posts can support a tree being espaliered, or trained to grow flat. A trellis mounted against a wall should be set 3 inches or more from it to allow ventilation and to prevent damage from reflected heat.

A trellis modeled after those used in commercial vineyards can be constructed from plastic-coated wire strung between T-shaped supports made of 2-by-4s and anchored to a wooden planter. Such a trellis is easily moved to provide optimum light conditions.

Trellis lathwork can be crisscrossed in the traditional diamond and rectangular weaves, in a free-form pattern, or set horizontally or vertically.

MATERIALS
Most trellises are made from strips of lath 1¼ inches wide. Other types of wood strips—grape stakes, battens or furring—can also be used, as can dowels ½ to 1 inch in diameter, commonly sold in 3-foot lengths. For a sturdier structure, use 1-by-2s, 1-by-4s or 2-by-4s.

Trellis kits containing ornate metal framework should not

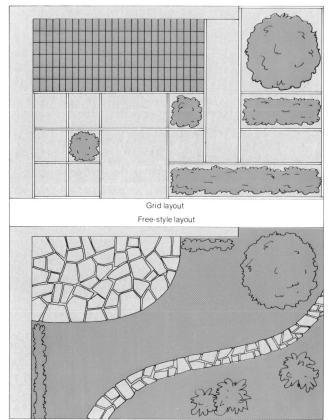

Grid layout
Free-style layout

TERRACE DESIGNS

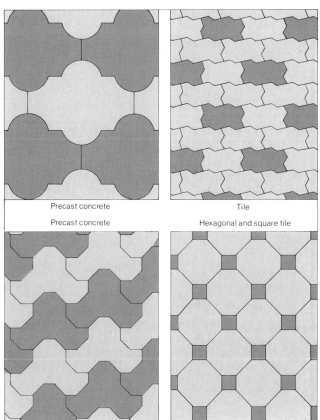

Precast concrete   Tile
Precast concrete   Hexagonal and square tile

PAVER AND TILE PATTERNS

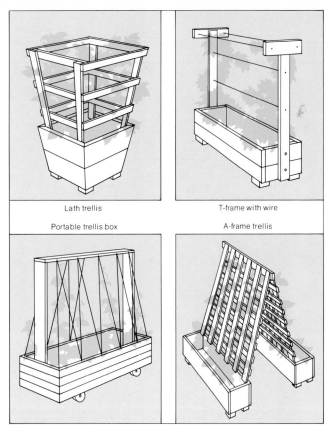

Lath trellis

Portable trellis box

T-frame with wire

A-frame trellis

TRELLISED PLANTERS

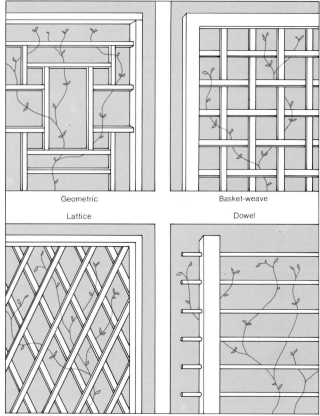

Geometric

Lattice

Basket-weave

Dowel

TRELLIS DESIGNS

be used; such framework absorbs heat that can injure tender vines. However, wire mesh and hardware cloth can be used to support plants with tendrils.

Soak lumber to be used in a trellis in a nontoxic wood preservative, or use a naturally rot- and insect-resistant wood like redwood or cedar. Assemble the trellis with galvanized fasteners and waterproof glue. The wood can be stained, if desired; painting is not recommended since plants must be removed every time repainting becomes necessary. Unfinished redwood and cedar will weather to a silvery gray color.

Walks

Walks connecting the house and various parts of the garden can define spaces within the yard, make movement easy from one area to another, and provide the gardener ready access to all parts of the garden with wheelbarrows, lawn mowers or other implements. A walk can be as simple as a wood-chip pathway or a grassy strip between flower beds. More often a walk is a durable surface designed for heavy traffic between such areas as the driveway and the house.

DESIGNS

In planning, consider 4 feet the minimum width for a walk. A walk that must accommodate two people side by side should be at least 5 feet wide. Do not overlook drainage. Combined with alternate freezing and thawing, poor drainage can cause paving to be heaved out of the ground and broken. Since clay or other heavy soils are the most difficult to drain, it may be necessary to install draintiles under a base of gravel, cinders or sand before building walks in such soils. In lighter soils, a base of loose aggregate alone is usually sufficient. To make sure that the walks will also shed water quickly, they should be set slightly above ground level and crowned so that water will drain to the sides. The center of a 5-foot walk, for example, should be about an inch higher than the edges.

Temporary paving, such as gravel or shredded bark, is generally contained between edging strips or headers made of wood or bricks. The walk area is excavated shallowly, a sheet of plastic is laid to inhibit weed growth, headers are installed and sand or gravel is spread evenly between them. Perforate the plastic at intervals to provide drainage.

In building a permanent walk of brick, flagstone or blocks, first outline the site, then excavate the area to accommodate both the drainage material and the paving. The paving may be laid dry without mortar on a well-drained base of 3 inches of gravel topped with a 1-inch layer of sand. Tamp each layer thoroughly and moisten the sand before positioning the bricks or blocks. Fill the cracks with more sand, sweeping it in at an angle to the joints. When paving with flagstone, keep in mind that the smaller the top surface of the stone, the thicker the stone must be for stability. When you are laying the stones, keep a straightedge along the outside of the walk, and place the larger stones toward the outer edge.

Brick, stone and block can also be mortared together on a concrete slab. Never mortar them without a solid base, however, or the walk will heave and crack. Whether a concrete slab is used as a base or as a finished surface, it should be at least 3 inches thick. If the concrete is used as a base, let it cure for at least 24 hours, then lay the paving material in a 1-inch bed of mortar. Tamp tiles or other paving materials lightly with a trowel handle until they are level; allow the mortar to cure for seven days before subjecting the walk to a heavy load. If the concrete is the final walk surface, finish it off in the desired texture and score contraction joints deeply at least every 8 feet to allow for settling and cracking.

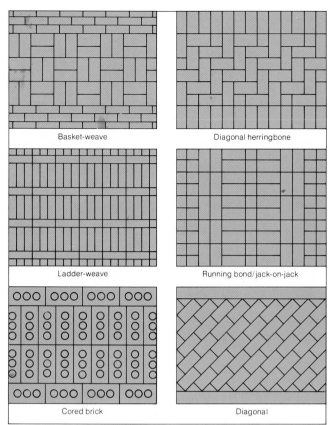

BRICK PATTERNS

Basket-weave

Diagonal herringbone

Ladder-weave

Running bond/jack-on-jack

Cored brick

Diagonal

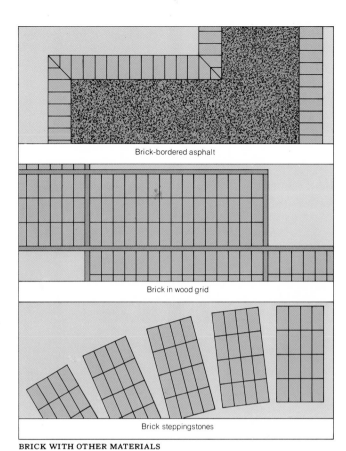

BRICK WITH OTHER MATERIALS

Brick-bordered asphalt

Brick in wood grid

Brick steppingstones

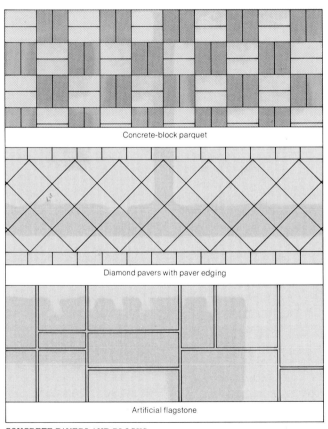

CONCRETE PAVERS AND BLOCKS

Concrete-block parquet

Diamond pavers with paver edging

Artificial flagstone

CONCRETE PAVERS WITH OTHER MATERIALS

Pavers with gravel aggregate

Pavers in grass

Pavers with pebbles

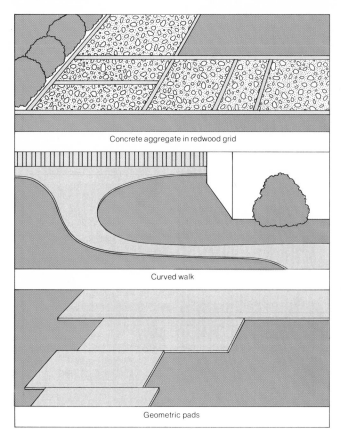

Concrete aggregate in redwood grid

Curved walk

Geometric pads

POURED CONCRETE

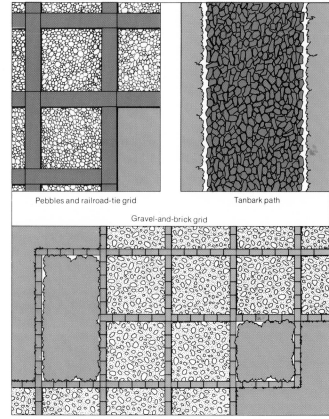

Pebbles and railroad-tie grid

Tanbark path

Gravel-and-brick grid

LOOSE PAVING MATERIALS

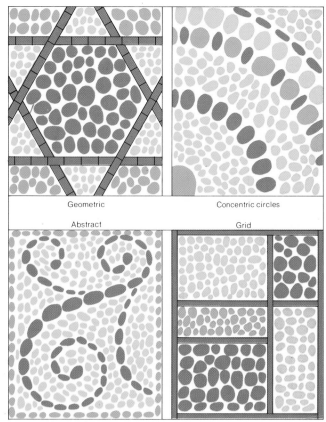

Geometric

Concentric circles

Abstract

Grid

PEBBLE AND STONE MOSAICS

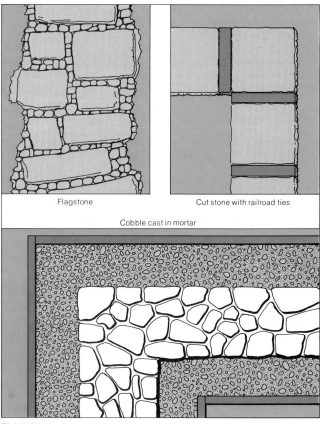

Flagstone

Cut stone with railroad ties

Cobble cast in mortar

FLAGSTONE AND STONE

MATERIALS

The great variety of paving materials available can generally be classified as temporary or permanent. Permanent pavings include bricks, blocks, concrete, asphalt, tile, flagstone and wood. Temporary pavings are loose materials that are useful for low-traffic areas, when a feeling of informality is desired or when you plan to build a more permanent walk later. Loose materials range from wood chips to rocks and gravel. Wood chips, bark chunks and shredded bark are popular organic paving materials that can do double duty as plant mulches. Loose inorganic materials like crushed rock, red rock, crushed brick and gravel are more costly than organic materials. They are available in chunks as large as an inch in diameter and as finely pulverized material that is laid down in two layers, each moistened and compacted.

Although temporary materials are less expensive than permanent paving, they must be replenished. Temporary pavings can also be difficult to walk on, may become weedy and, if used next to a lawn, can create a hazard when mowing.

The choice of paving material for a walk should be influenced by the amount of traffic expected, climatic conditions and harmony with its surroundings. Frequently used walks require a material that is easy to walk on, provides sure footing, does not become slick when wet, cleans easily, does not get tracked into the house in wet weather and does not require frequent repair or replacement. Weather conditions such as snow, frost, heavy rainfall or extreme temperatures may dictate the exclusion of some materials or designs.

Both the paving material chosen and the design into which it is incorporated contribute to the effect the walk creates in the landscape. Wood rounds or steppingstones placed off-center impart an informal look, while bricks laid in symmetrical patterns conjure up images of formal colonial gardens. Wood makes a more permanent walk than loose materials but is not as long lasting as masonry and will eventually rot. It is best used in dry climates or on top of a 4- to 6-inch layer of drainage material. Choose naturally rot-resistant woods or those that have been treated with wood preservatives.

The color, texture and pattern of any paving material should harmonize with the house as well as the landscape. Brick, small in scale, is effective in repetitive patterns, as is tile. Concrete is a versatile material, and walks that are made of it need not be limited to cement-gray. Concrete can be colored, textured and formed in almost any shape. Pebble mosaics set in concrete can turn a walk into a work of art.

Walls

Once used mainly for fortification, freestanding walls now serve more benign functions. Like fences, they can define property lines, screen out unsightly views, act as windbreaks, muffle noises and create shade. Low walls often add bonus seating to outdoor living areas. Retaining walls on sloping sites create level areas and prevent soil from washing away.

DESIGNS

Since a wall is a permanent and usually dominant outdoor structure, great care should be taken in coordinating design with material. The size of a wall and the material that is used in it should be in scale with other nearby structures and landscape features. Concrete blocks are larger in size and scale than bricks, for example, and thus are less suitable than bricks for low walls. The color, pattern and texture of the wall material and design should also be compatible with the surroundings. Contrasting materials used in part of a design can relieve monotony, but combinations must be made judiciously. Ridged blocks will create interesting shadow pat-

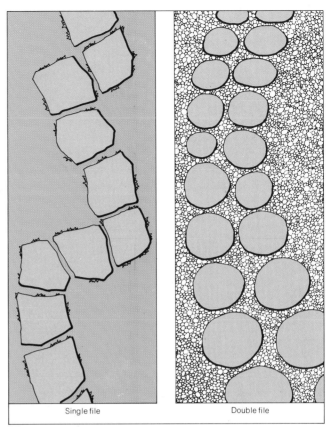

Single file | Double file

STEPPINGSTONE

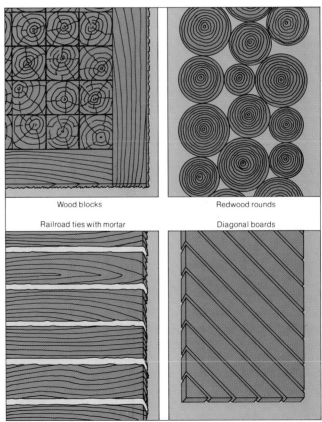

Wood blocks | Redwood rounds
Railroad ties with mortar | Diagonal boards

WOOD WALKS

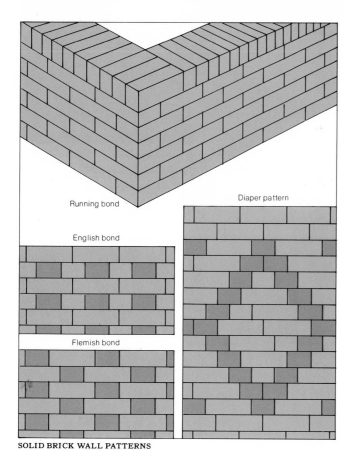

SOLID BRICK WALL PATTERNS

Running bond
Diaper pattern
English bond
Flemish bond

Roman brick
Serpentine retaining wall
Capped wall

SOLID BRICK WALLS

terns; bricks and blocks can be laid in patterns that create the same effect. Where a high masonry wall is not practical, a low wall can be topped with a lightweight fence.

Choose the site of the wall carefully, avoiding large trees whose strong, wide-ranging roots could damage footings. Early in the planning of a property-line wall, make sure you will not be encroaching on a neighbor's property. If you have any doubts, have your lot surveyed. (Many gardeners build walls a foot or two inside property lines to allow easy maintenance access.) Check local building codes for any restrictions that may affect height, material, size, setback and footing and for the necessity of obtaining a building permit. After the preliminary checks, plan the wall's thickness, height, reinforcement, footing, slope or taper, and coping.

The thickness, height and reinforcement of a wall are interrelated. With a sound foundation, a brick wall only 1 to 2 feet high can be a single brick thick—about 4 inches. Taller walls or retaining and seat walls built of brick should be two or three bricks thick and reinforced with vertical steel rods. (A serpentine wall is an exception; although only a single brick thick, it can be built as high as 6 feet without reinforcement, gaining stability from its curving design.) Concrete-block walls up to 4 feet tall can be built one standard block thick without reinforcement; higher walls need the added support of vertical rods. Freestanding walls of reinforced cast concrete 4 to 6 inches thick can rise 6 feet or more. Mortared ashlar stone walls up to 4 feet tall should be 8 to 18 inches thick, while mortarless rubble stone walls, called dry walls, must have a base thickness equal to half their height.

A footing provides a solid foundation and an even base for any wall. Footings should rest on firm ground below the frost line if possible (map, page 143). Poured-concrete foundations provide the most stable base. Even in warm climates where frost heaving is not a problem, the soil may be so unstable that footings are needed. Brick walls less than a foot high can be laid in mortar on a poured-concrete foundation or on a bed of sand 6 to 8 inches deep. Taller brick walls or those built of concrete blocks need concrete footings that extend twice the thickness of the wall below the frost line.

Concrete footings for brick walls should cure for 24 to 48 hours before the bricks are laid, while concrete blocks can be set on either a wet or a dry foundation; the wet foundation method (the concrete still somewhat soft) produces a sturdier wall but is difficult for the amateur since the first course must be completed before the concrete sets. Poured-concrete walls require a footing twice the width of the wall. Dry stone walls are usually set on a bed of sand 5 to 6 inches deep.

Stone walls taper from the base to the top. Freestanding mortared stone walls usually slope inward 1 inch for every foot of height; dry stone walls need a slope of 1 to 2 inches for every foot of height; stone retaining walls need a slope of at least 8 to 10 inches for every 5 feet of height.

Masonry walls need a coping, or cap, at the top to give them a finished appearance and to keep water from seeping into and damaging the masonry or mortar. The coping usually extends at least an inch beyond the wall on both sides. Cast-concrete walls can be capped with a stiff mortar curved with a template; a masonry sealer can also be used.

Building a solid, safe retaining wall that will not overturn or slide forward, especially during rainy weather, is no easy task. A low retaining wall (3 feet or less) that will not be under great stress can be built by an amateur. For a taller structure, it is advisable to seek the help of a professional. The most important consideration in constructing a retaining wall is to provide for adequate drainage, either through or around the wall. Ditches, gutters, weep holes and draintiles

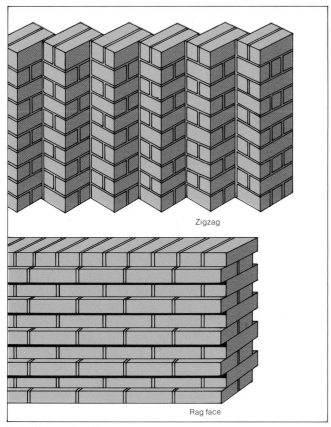

Zigzag

Rag face

SOLID BRICK WALLS

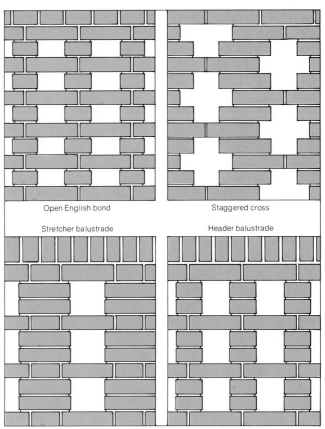

Open English bond

Staggered cross

Stretcher balustrade

Header balustrade

PIERCED BRICK WALLS

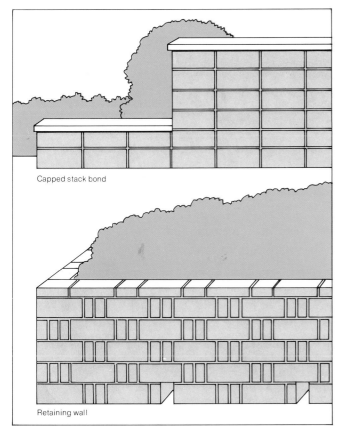

Capped stack bond

Retaining wall

CONCRETE-BLOCK WALLS

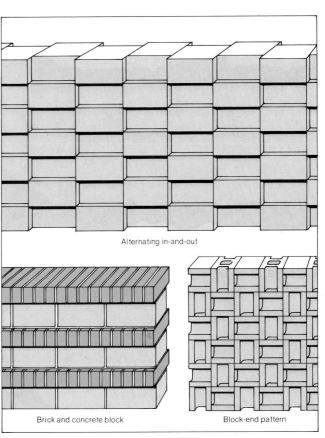

Alternating in-and-out

Brick and concrete block

Block-end pattern

CONCRETE-BLOCK WALLS

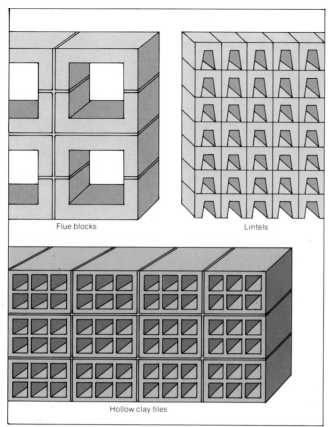

CONCRETE AND TILE GRILLES

Flue blocks

Lintels

Hollow clay tiles

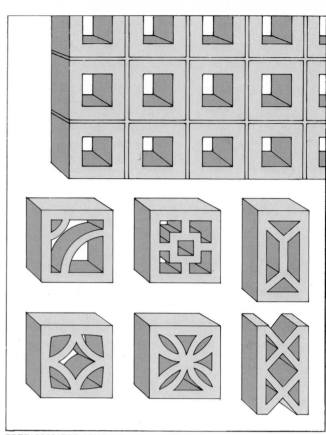

PREFABRICATED CONCRETE SCREEN BLOCKS

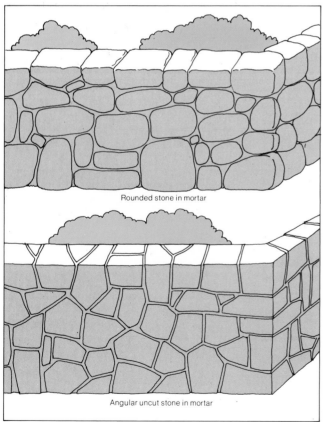

Rounded stone in mortar

Angular uncut stone in mortar

RUBBLE STONE WALLS

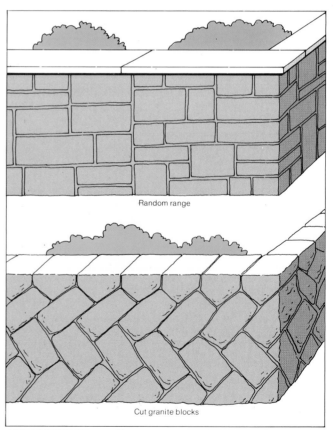

Random range

Cut granite blocks

ASHLAR STONE WALLS

must be incorporated into the design. When retaining walls are expected to hold back substantial amounts of heavy, wet soil, special anchors called "dead men" are installed so they extend into the soil behind the wall.

The first step in building a brick or block wall is to lay out the wall line with stakes and string. Then dig a foundation trench twice as wide as the wall width. If you are using footings of poured concrete, prepare the wood forms first, then pour and level the concrete, insert vertical reinforcing rods and let the concrete set. Before beginning actual construction, lay out a test course (one layer of bricks or blocks) on the foundation to check fit and alignment. Remove this course and lightly spray the foundation and the bricks or blocks with a garden hose. Secure the first course with mortar and check to be sure it is level.

Build up the corners first, stepping them down toward the center. Attach a guide line to keep the courses straight and level and check for plumb every three or four courses. Use a mortar that is carefully made, with ingredients measured accurately and mixed thoroughly. Put down a small amount of mortar at a time, covering the abutting surfaces of bricks, stones or blocks. Tap each piece level with a trowel handle and check with a taut string. Scrape off excess mortar. Space around vertical reinforcing rods should be mortared at each level. If work on the wall must be interrupted, cover completed work with a tarpaulin or plastic sheet. As the wall is constructed, you may want to attach gate fittings. (Hinge bolts can be set right in the mortar joints as you are building the wall; the bolts will be anchored more firmly than if they were sunk into pilot holes made after the mortar has hardened.) Attach the top course and smooth the joints along the face of the wall to a desired shape. Wet down the completed wall and keep it moist for several days until the mortar has cured. Then clean off mortar stains and drippings with a solution of 1 part muriatic acid to 9 parts water; wear rubber gloves while applying the solution with a stiff-bristled brush.

Casting a concrete wall is similar to casting a footing. In both cases, the forms should be thoroughly coated with oil so they can be easily removed when the concrete has hardened.

MATERIALS

Brick, block, stone and poured concrete are most frequently used in constructing masonry walls. Straight or curving brick walls can be built in a variety of attractive patterns. The relatively small and uniform size of bricks makes them easy to work with, but they require more construction time than larger units. A multitude of patterns is possible when walls of concrete blocks are constructed in various colors, shapes, sizes and textures. Their larger size makes construction go more quickly, but since they weigh up to 50 pounds each, concrete blocks can be awkward to handle.

Natural or shaped stones can be laid either dry or with mortar. Construction is a challenge, however, because of the uneven shape, size and weight of the stones. Poured concrete can be used in any design for which a form can be constructed, but to be safe, walls higher than 3 feet require professional skill and the use of heavy equipment. Among wood products, railroad ties, timbers and utility poles are all used for retaining walls.

Coping materials used to cap a masonry wall include special coping blocks, bricks laid in a soldier course (with their narrow ends exposed), flagstone, cast concrete and wood.

WATERING See Sprinkler Systems
WINDBREAKS See Fences, Walls
WORK CENTERS See Storage

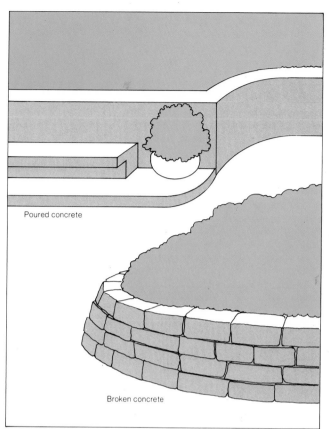

Poured concrete

Broken concrete

CONCRETE WALLS

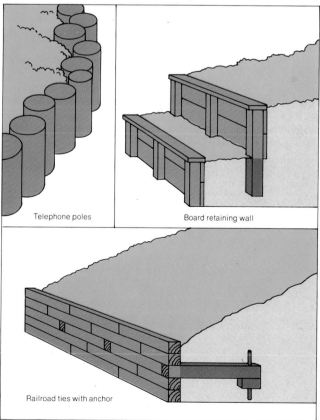

Telephone poles

Board retaining wall

Railroad ties with anchor

WOOD WALLS

Characteristics of 27 materials

Carefully chosen designs for garden projects (page 111) will go for nought if inappropriate building materials are used. A material may be inappropriate for esthetic reasons—perhaps too rough in size or texture where delicacy is more in order, or so garish in color that it commands undue attention. But a material is more likely to be inappropriate because it will not survive the garden environment: sun, wind, rain, freezing, thawing. Some materials are naturally weather-resistant; others can be made so with special treatment. Characteristics to consider as you select materials are discussed here.

Adobe

A building-block material made of clay soil and water, with straw sometimes added to give strength, is called adobe. An asphalt stabilizer is commonly added to retard weathering, but this greatly increases the cost. Structures of any size can be built with these molded, sun-dried blocks, one of the oldest construction materials known. Adobe bricks are used in terrace floors.

Common in the U.S. only in the Southwest where soil of the right composition is found, adobe bricks and blocks are so heavy (12 to 45 pounds each) that the cost of transporting them to other regions is prohibitive. Furthermore, adobe without stabilizing asphalt can be used only in an arid or semiarid climate; frequent hard rain would melt it away. But it lasts indefinitely if it stays dry, as Indian relics attest.

Adobe bricks and blocks are sold regionally at manufacturing plants, where you also can buy clay soil by the cubic yard for use in mortaring and plastering. The blocks commonly are 4 by 16 inches across their faces and from 3½ to 12 inches deep; the bricks are 6 by 12 or 12 by 12 inches and are usually 2½ inches thick.

Walls built of adobe are laid in courses like other brickwork and require strong foundations and, if higher than 2 feet, steel reinforcement as required by the local building code. Paving bricks are set on a bed of sand. Since dimensions can vary from block to block and brick to brick, tight-fitting patterns are not appropriate.

AGGREGATE See Concrete, Sand, Stone

Aluminum

Aluminum building materials are such relative newcomers that many people still object to having them in a garden. But there is no denying aluminum's many advantages over more traditional materials. Aluminum is lightweight, extremely strong for its weight, easily worked and almost maintenance-free. Readily cut with ordinary tin snips, a hack saw or a power saw with a metal-cutting blade, aluminum products are easy to shape and install, though gloves and goggles are advisable if power tools are used. Over a long period of years, aluminum is more economical than most other building materials.

Among the products available for garden projects are aluminum lath, insect screening, threaded rods, louvered sun screening and panels that are flat, corrugated, crimped or perforated for use in fences, overhead structures and storage buildings. Many products are finished with baked-on paint that resists chipping, peeling or blistering. Also available are fencing panels and posts that mimic familiar patterns: the gothic picket, board-and-board, basket-weave and other designs.

Asbestos board

Of all materials available for outdoor construction, asbestos board is one of the most durable. The flat or corrugated sheets made of cement and asbestos fiber are used for fences, windbreaks and overhead structures where a long, maintenance-free life is important. Asbestos board is impervious to fire, corrosion, weathering and pest attacks. It may be primed and painted, but if left its natural cement-gray color it needs no maintenance at all. The durability and low maintenance are offset by its relatively high cost and brittleness.

The sheets come in standard widths of 42 or 48 inches and lengths of 4, 8, 10 and 12 feet. Panels ⅜ to ½ inch thick are recommended for outdoor use. The sheets can be cut, using a tungsten-carbide saw blade; they can also be snapped like pieces of glass after being scored on both sides. Drill all fastening holes before beginning installation. Weighing 2 to 4 pounds per square foot, depending on the thickness, asbestos board is a heavy material that requires strong supporting posts.

Since the asbestos fibers are locked into the boards by cement, asbestos board presents no health hazard until it is cut. If you cut or drill it, work in an area that has good ventilation and wear a face mask with a filter to avoid inhaling any loose fibers.

Asphalt

Asphalt is a tarlike substance that becomes a durable paving material when mixed with gravel and sand. Properly installed asphalt surfaces are almost as durable as those made of concrete or bricks and considerably less expensive than either. Unlike concrete, asphalt is easily patched if the soil beneath it sags or heaves, causing cracks. But poorly mixed and compacted asphalt can become a nightmare of sticky shoes and crumbling edges. Because the dark color absorbs heat, an asphalt terrace can be uncomfortably warm unless it is well shaded. Still, asphalt paving is an economical choice for such large areas as tennis courts, driveways, service yards or long garden paths.

TYPES. The most durable kind of asphalt is hot-mixed asphaltic concrete. A combination of hot asphalt and gravel that is factory-mixed and delivered by truck, it is applied as a liquid that hardens as it cools. Proper installation requires professional skill and equipment.

Cold-mix asphalt is a mixture of aggregates and asphalt suspended in a liquid. After the mix is spread and compacted, it hardens slowly as the liquid evaporates. Designated by grades as slow, medium or fast according to its hardening speed, cold-mix asphalt is available at building-supply and hardware stores in 60- to 100-pound bags for patching or surfacing small areas. It may take months to harden completely.

Emulsified liquid asphalt is poured over a gravel base. Available in bulk and relatively easy to use, it hardens so quickly its best use is in small areas.

INSTALLATION. For asphalt paving, first excavate, grade and compact a soil bed where the paving will go. Treat the soil with a weed killer to keep plants from growing through the asphalt later. Build wooden forms to establish the shape, drainage and thickness of the asphalt—generally 1½ to 2 inches for a driveway, 1 to 1½ inches for walks and terraces. Plan to leave the forms in place permanently to prevent crumbling edges. In regions where the soil freezes, compact a 3- to 4-inch subbase of sand or other fine aggregate. Then spread on the asphalt mix and roll it firmly. The wet surface can be finished by brushing sand or pea gravel over it and rolling it in. Hardened asphalt can be colored with special plastic paints.

BEAMS See Wood
BLOCK See Adobe, Concrete, Glass, Stone
BOLTS See Fasteners

Brick

Some 5,000 years ago, man discovered that a hard, durable material could be made by baking clay in a mold. The bricks that resulted have been a popular building material ever since. Bricks have become available in more than 10,000 combinations of color, shape, size and texture. Despite such variety, most can be classified as common, face or paving bricks.

COMMON. The most economical for garden use are common bricks, also called building or sewer bricks. Usually red, they measure 7½ to 8 inches long, 2¼ inches thick and 3¼ to 3½ inches wide. Three kinds of common bricks that are frequently used in garden construction are wire-cut, sand-mold and clinker. Wire-cut bricks are straight-sided, rough-textured and often pitted. Smoother sand-mold bricks are turned out in molds so the top face is slightly larger than the bottom. Clinker bricks, also called hard-burned, are the toughest; they are often overbaked, causing black patches and surface irregularities, so clinker bricks are used where they will not show.

FACE. More expensive for garden-construction projects, face bricks are sometimes used to make decorative walls, walks and planters.

Most face bricks are made with holes in them to make them lighter. If these are used for paving, they will last longer if they are set on edge.

CHOOSING BRICK FACING

After you have decided on a size and grade of brick for a garden wall or paving, you have a choice of many different surface textures. For walls, esthetics are generally the only considerations, and any of the six types of facings shown below will do. Paving requires additional attributes: it must be both safe and comfortable to walk on; because of their uneven surfaces, stippled, rug and water-struck bricks are rarely used underfoot.

COMMON BUILDING BRICK

RUG BRICK

SMOOTH BRICK

SAND-FINISHED BRICK

STIPPLED BRICK

WATER-STRUCK BRICK

SIZING UP BRICKS

Bricks are available in a wide variety of sizes and shapes, from elegant, narrow Roman bricks to oversized utility bricks. Cored bricks are not weaker, as might be supposed, but are lighter and easier to handle. The dimensions of the modular bricks listed below are nominal, including allowance for a mortar joint.

Standard brick—4 × 2⅔ × 8

Engineer brick—4 × 3⅕ × 8

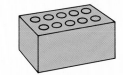
Economy brick—4 × 4 × 8

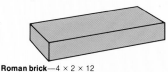
Roman brick—4 × 2 × 12

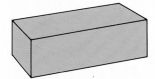
Utility brick—4 × 4 × 12

Cored brick—6 × 2⅔ ×12

PAVING. Solid paving bricks are particularly durable underfoot in the garden. They are available in such colors as brown, yellow and pink as well as red. Paving bricks are slightly larger than common bricks. Special paving bricks only 1¼ inches thick are sometimes available and are set in place with mortar like tiles. Paving bricks have a rough texture for good traction and to reduce glare.

Paving and face bricks are available with various textures on the side that will be exposed to view, including rug, which is striped with deep grooves; sand-finished, with grit embedded; stippled, with a rough, mottled look; and water-struck, with an etched, sculptural appearance.

OTHER BRICKS. Used bricks, reclaimed from old buildings and cleaned of mortar, have a worn and weathered appearance difficult to duplicate artificially. Such reclaimed bricks can be used in walls or for paving but they should be set on concrete bases.

Fire bricks are made to withstand very high temperatures. They are used in the garden to line barbecue pits.

BUYING BRICKS. All bricks are graded according to their weather resistance. Bricks rated NW do not have weather-resistant qualities and are for interior use only. Bricks rated MW (moderate weathering) can be used outdoors where only a few days of freezing temperatures occur. Bricks rated SW (severe weathering) can be used in contact with the ground in very cold regions.

When you order bricks, add 5 per cent to your calculated needs to allow for breakage and replacement. Five standard bricks set tightly without mortar will cover 1 square foot, as will four and one half bricks set with a ½-inch mortar joint. Bricks are commonly sold in 500- and 1,000-brick cubes. Buying bricks in such standard lots is economical and ensures that they will be roughly the same color and size, although bricks within the same lot can vary in size as much as 3 per cent.

BUILDING ANCHORS See Fasteners

Canvas

Tightly woven cotton or acrylic canvas, available in a number of weaves, finishes and weights, may last up to 10 years outdoors. The types commonly used include heavy-duty army duck and lightweight drill. Vat-dyed canvas is the least expensive but is not as colorfast as vinyl-laminated or acrylic-coated canvas. Vinyl-laminated canvas is also more resistant to soiling. Most manufacturers treat canvas with fire-resistant and mildew-proof chemicals; both are highly desirable.

Canvas weighing from 6 to 18 ounces a linear yard is sold at awning stores in 31-, 36- or 54-inch-wide rolls. Ten-ounce canvas is suitable for awnings and overheads, 8-ounce is used for porch umbrellas and 6- to 8-ounce fabric is made into furniture covers.

When you work with new canvas, allow for a shrinkage of 3 inches in each linear yard. Sew with extra-strength polyester thread, since cotton may rot. Ten-ounce canvas is the heaviest that a home sewing machine can handle.

Mildew is the worst enemy of canvas. Be sure that awnings and umbrellas are completely dry after rain before they are folded. Before canvas coverings are taken in for the winter, they should be hosed with cold water, scrubbed with a soft brush and dried while they are on the frames. Store canvas in a cool, dry, well-ventilated area protected from rodents.

Carpeting (outdoor)

Most indoor-outdoor carpeting is suitable only for use on porches, terraces

---

METHODS OF CURING FRESH CONCRETE

Fresh concrete must be cured by being kept moist for several days. Water starts a chemical reaction that bonds the ingredients of the concrete, so that the longer you cure it the stronger it will be—a week is generally sufficient. The table below evaluates techniques for curing fresh concrete.

Technique	Advantages	Disadvantages
WAYS TO ADD WATER:		
1. Covering with a pool of water	Insulates and gives optimum results	Usable only on flat surfaces
2. Sprinkling by hand or hose	Inexpensive and works well if done regularly	May dry between sprinklings; walls drain too quickly
3. Covering with burlap or matting	Works well if kept constantly wet	May dry out
4. Covering with straw, sand or earth	Inexpensive and insulates from cold	May dry out; difficult to remove; earth may leave stain
WAYS TO KEEP WATER IN:		
1. Applying chemical curing compounds	Works well and permits lengthy curing	Usually requires sprayer; rain may wash off; weak insulator
2. Covering with plastic film	Watertight and easy to handle	Must be weighted down; may cause discoloring
3. Covering with waterproof paper	Works well if tightly overlapped at edges	Usable only on horizontal surfaces; expensive and hard to handle

and decks that have roofs to provide partial shelter from the elements. However, "turf" carpeting made of polypropylene olefin fibers—the type used to cover football fields—is durable enough to withstand any kind of weather.

Turf carpeting has a rubber or vinyl backing. Available in 6- and 12-foot widths, it comes in a wide range of colors and patterns as well as the familiar green. Several grades are sold by the square yard by carpet retailers. It can be rolled out loose or installed with adhesives on any well-drained, hard surface. It needs only an occasional sweeping and hosing to keep it clean.

Cement

Portland cement is a bonding agent that is combined in various proportions with lime, water and aggregates such as sand and gravel to make concrete, mortar and stucco.

"Portland" is not a brand name but a type of cement produced according to strict standards. Its English inventor, Joseph Aspdin, named his mixture for its supposed resemblance, when cast, to the fine limestone quarried on the English Isle of Portland. The cement is a free-flowing powder made of minerals obtained in large part from limestone.

Building-material dealers sell portland cement in moistureproof paper bags weighing 94 pounds and measuring 1 cubic foot. Do not buy broken bags; moisture absorbed from the air will ruin the cement.

Epoxy and latex cements are used to patch old stucco or concrete. Epoxy mixed with sand and cement makes an extremely strong patching compound, but like all epoxy products, the elements must be combined just before the compound is needed and any leftover mixture must be discarded. Latex

cement can make a repair that is all but undetectable. It is sold in 5-, 10- or 40-pound bags of dry cement and latex to which water is added or as separate cans of liquid latex and powder.

CHAIN LINK See Wire fencing
CINDER BLOCKS See Concrete

Concrete

A mixture of portland cement, water and an aggregate such as sand, gravel, crushed rock, vermiculite or cinders, concrete is used in garden projects in liquid form that can be shaped and smoothed before it hardens or as precast concrete blocks used like bricks.

POURED CONCRETE. Dry ready-mix formulations for making concrete, packaged in the proper proportions, are handy for small projects. You simply add water and mix, usually with a hoe

FROZEN WATER: THE UNDERGROUND ENEMY

Water in the soil nourishes all plants in mild weather, but when the water freezes, it can cause serious damage to fence posts, wall footings and paving blocks.

Freezing water expands, moving the surrounding soil. When the ice thaws, the soil is subjected to further disturbance. To prevent this damage, footings and posts should rest on stable soil beneath the frost line—that is, the deepest level of frost penetration. Bricks

and other pavers can float on top of a base of sand or poured concrete if you use grades of brick that are matched to the frost conditions in your area.

As shown on the accompanying frost-line map prepared by the U.S. Weather Bureau, the depth of the frost line varies in this country from an inch in northern Florida to 72 inches in northern Maine.

Altitude, weather patterns and composition

of soil also affect frost-line depth. Thus, in relatively flat states, frost depths are fairly uniform, but in the upper midwestern and western states, the patterns vary greatly because of mountain ranges or soil diversity.

Local building codes generally are a good indication of the depth of the frost line, although in some areas the codes may require deeper footings than the depth of the frost alone would necessitate.

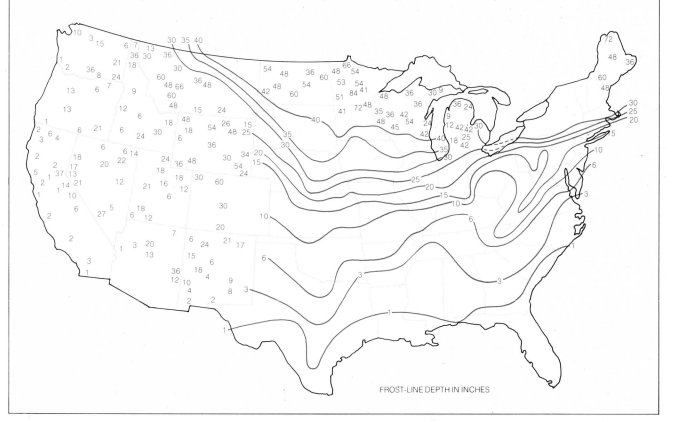

FROST-LINE DEPTH IN INCHES

in a metal wheelbarrow. For somewhat larger projects, it is more economical to buy the ingredients separately, either mixing them by hand or in a rented portable power mixer. For very large projects, such as a terrace or a driveway, you can buy transit-mixed concrete, poured from the truck that mixes it and delivers it to the site. Such dealers usually will deliver only a cubic yard or more. Transit-mix concrete must be poured and smoothed rapidly; prepare excavations and forms in advance, and have helpers on hand with the necessary rakes, shovels, floats and trowels to level the mix.

CONCRETE BLOCKS. There are more than 1,000 choices of patterns and textures in concrete blocks. As building blocks, they are inexpensive and are good insulators against cold and noise. Most have hollow cores but are still heavy; handle them carefully to avoid muscle strain. Concrete blocks are virtually maintenance-free.

The most common sizes of concrete blocks are 8 by 8 by 16 inches, weighing 40 to 50 pounds, and 4 by 8 by 16 inches, weighing 25 to 30 pounds. In both cases, the actual dimensions are ⅜ inch less than the nominal dimensions, which allows space for a mortar joint.

Concrete blocks are formulated to suit particular climate conditions. Type II is suitable for most areas, but Type I is recommended for very dry climates where Type II blocks might shrink and crack. A lightweight 8-by-8-by-16-inch concrete block, made with vermiculite or cinder aggregate instead of gravel, weighs about 25 pounds.

Split blocks are long and thin with rough faces. Slump blocks, which sag slightly when removed from their mold, resemble stone. Glazed blocks resemble tile. A range of colored blocks is available in some areas, although all blocks that are not glazed are easily painted.

Various patterns of grillwork and screen blocks can be laid on edge in a wall to provide ventilation and a decorative pattern. Special surface textures, too, are available for decorative use.

Concrete block walls 4 feet high or more are laid on a foundation of concrete poured over vertical steel reinforcement rods that give extra strength. The thin, solid concrete blocks used to cap a wall can also be used as paving blocks, set on a bed of sand and held in place with header boards.

Fasteners

NAILS. Formed from wire or cut from metal plates, nails are the quickest and simplest fasteners to use for joining wood. Aluminum or stainless steel nails are preferable for outdoor use since even galvanized nails may rust.

Nail lengths are usually designated in "pennies," abbreviated "d." Most kinds of nails range from 2d (about 1 inch) to 60d (about 6 inches). Those commonly used in garden construction are shown in the table opposite. Use nails two and a half to three times longer than the width of the board you are nailing for the strongest joint.

SCREWS. With their threaded shanks, screws make stronger joints than nails and are especially useful if the lumber is not thick enough to hold a nail securely. Decorative screwheads are preferable where fasteners are exposed.

Screws are classified by both length and gauge; the higher the gauge, the thicker the screw. The heads of the screws may be flat, round or oval, and may have either conventional straight screwdriver slots or the cross-shaped Phillips-head slots. All are available in a great variety of rust-resistant and decorative finishes. Choose a screw whose length is two thirds the total thickness of the boards being joined. Screws with fine threads are best for

BLOCKS FOR EVERY PURPOSE

Several kinds of cinder blocks and concrete blocks are available for gardening projects. The stretcher block is the most common type; its hollow cores and end projections assure strong mortar joints. A corner block is identical to the stretcher except that one end is flat so it can be left exposed. A half block is used to start a running-bond pattern of staggered vertical joints. Partition and half-height blocks are used to provide weep holes in retaining walls for drainage. Coreless blocks and solid-top blocks are used where cores would be unsightly, as in the caps of walls and planters. Screen blocks, of which three representative types are illustrated, are used to build airy, decorative walls and partitions.

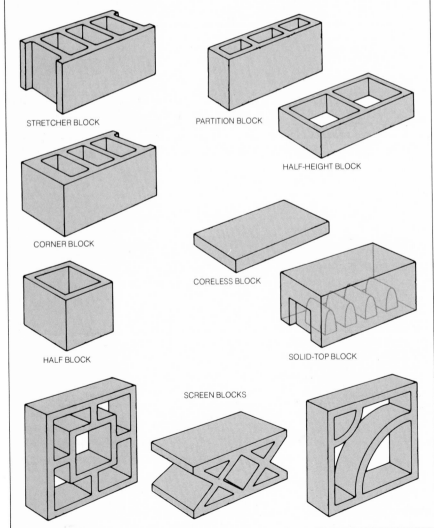

STRETCHER BLOCK

PARTITION BLOCK

HALF-HEIGHT BLOCK

CORNER BLOCK

CORELESS BLOCK

HALF BLOCK

SOLID-TOP BLOCK

SCREEN BLOCKS

FASTENERS FOR EVERY NEED

The fasteners that are commonly used for garden construction and general carpentry are illustrated here. Some, like nails, can be used for a variety of jobs, while other fasteners, such as toggle bolts and post caps, are intended for specific purposes.

NAILS

Available in a range of lengths for an endless variety of jobs, the nails shown are measured by inches and by penny ratings. As a general rule, a nail should be three times as long as the thickness of the wood being secured.

Common nail. Made with a broad head, it will not pull through a board.

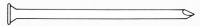

Siding nail. Used to fasten exterior siding; head can be countersunk.

Finishing nail. Used for fine work; head is sunk, then covered with wood filler.

Masonry nail. Forged from tempered steel, it is used to join wood to masonry.

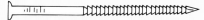

Annular-ring nail. Ridges lock into wood, giving great strength.

WOOD SCREWS

Used where joints will be subject to stress, screws hold more firmly than nails. They are sold by diameter, length, type of metal and type of head.

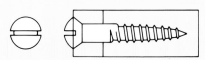

Oval-head screw. Tapered shoulder can be partially countersunk for holding power.

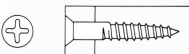

Phillips-head screw. Double slot reduces slippage. Heads may be flat, oval or round.

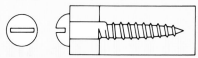

Round-head screw. Head will not penetrate wood. Often used in temporary structures.

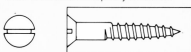

Flat-head screw. Preferred where screw will be invisible; head is fully countersunk.

BOLTS

Threaded rods that are usually tightened in place by turning a companion nut, bolts are used for heavy-duty work. Sizes are designated by diameter and by the number of threads per inch of length.

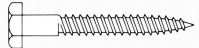

Lag bolt. Pointed screw end is driven into fixed joints in places where it is impossible to use a nut.

Carriage bolt. Made with a shoulder to prevent turning as nut is tightened. Sold with round or countersunk head.

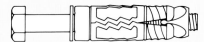

Masonry bolt and anchor. As the hexagonal head is turned, the sheath around it expands to grip the inside of a predrilled hole.

Toggle bolt. Used to secure object to a hollow wall. Spring-tension wings open to grip wall as bolt is turned.

Molly bolt. A hollow-wall anchor, it is encased in a sheath that opens to grip the wall as the bolt head is turned.

Turnbuckle. Tightens wire used to support gate or fence post. Sleeve is turned to increase or decrease tension.

ANCHORS

These metal connectors hold more securely than bolts. When they are carefully attached and painted, they blend unobtrusively with most wooden structures. Following are three common types of anchors.

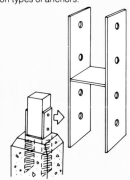

Post anchor. Used to join a post to a concrete footing or slab.

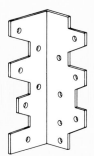

Framing anchor. Used to connect a corner joint that is not load bearing.

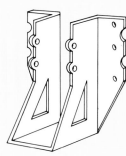

Joist anchor. Used to join a joist or rafter to a beam or ledger in a tight, flush connection.

OTHER JOINT REINFORCERS

These special hardware devices are used for stronger connections than those provided by nails, bolts or screws alone.

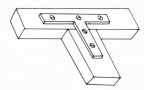

T plate. A sturdy connector for joining wood at a spot other than an end or a corner.

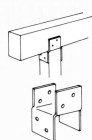

Post cap. Used to connect a post to a beam, particularly where toenailing is not practical.

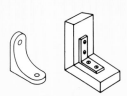

Corner brace. Used for extra support of a load-bearing joint.

hardwoods; those with coarse threads bind softwoods more tightly.

BOLTS. Use bolts where the strongest holding power is required. Although some bolts have self-tapping threads, most are inserted through predrilled holes and secured with nuts. Cadmium-plated bolts stand up best to outdoor moisture. The bolt's length should be the thickness of both lumber pieces plus ½ inch. Use a ¼-inch diameter bolt for lumber up to 2 inches thick; a ⅜-inch diameter for 3-inch lumber; a ½-inch diameter for 4-inch lumber.

Expansion bolts are used to fasten wood to plaster or masonry. A plug is placed in a hole drilled in the masonry with a carbide-tipped drill; it expands and tightens against the sides of the hole as the bolt is driven into it.

ADHESIVES. Glues and mastics are useful for securing odd-shaped joints, for reinforcing nailed constructions and for joining wood to masonry. Powdered or liquid epoxy-resin glues and pre-mixed mastics especially made for outdoor use will not be affected by rain and temperature changes.

METAL CONNECTORS. Galvanized fasteners such as post caps, flat braces of various shapes (L, T, Y or H, for example), framing anchors and metal clips are used where nailing is difficult or will not provide sufficient joint strength. Post anchors and other types of masonry-to-wood connectors are embedded in masonry as it is being constructed or are attached to the finished masonry surfaces.

Finishes

Depending on the effect desired, outdoor wood surfaces can be stained, painted or given a clear finish. Special stains and paints are available for use on outdoor masonry.

CLEAR FINISH. Natural weathering is often preferred for outdoor structures made of a rot-resistant wood like redwood or cedar, or a softwood that has been pressure-treated with a wood preservative. Most such woods weather to soft shades of tan to gray with varying amounts of sheen. The aging process can be simulated by using a mild caustic solution on the wood. New redwood, for example, can be darkened by brushing it with a solution of 1 part baking soda to 10 parts water.

If some protection against weathering is desired, use a clear sealer such as linseed oil, spar (marine) varnish or a clear penetrating finish. For best penetration, thin linseed oil with mineral spirits and apply several coats. Similarly, several applications of thinned marine varnish will reduce the tendency of the varnish to crack or peel outdoors. A clear penetrating finish needs renewal about every five years.

STAINS. The pigmented formulations called stains penetrate and color wood without obscuring its texture or grain. Stains are available in a wide variety of colors, some more transparent than others. Some nonchalking sealer-type stains contain ingredients that inhibit mildew. A gallon of stain will cover 350 to 400 square feet. Before applying stain, pretreat bare wood with a clear penetrating wood preservative. Carefully applied stains will last five to seven years before restaining is needed.

Special stains are made for use on old concrete surfaces or on new concrete that has cured at least six weeks. One gallon covers about 400 square feet, and two coats are usually needed.

PAINT. To get an opaque colored film on a wood surface, use paint. Available in either flat, semigloss or gloss finish, paint is the most moisture-resistant finish available for wood and offers the widest choice of colors.

Latex paint is a water-soluble formulation of pigment suspended in a natural or synthetic resin base. The quickest to dry of the exterior paints, it stretches and shrinks with temperature changes, thereby resisting cracking and peeling. Easy-to-apply alkyd paint, also resin-based, offers higher gloss and brighter colors than latex but dries very slowly. Oil paint contains pigment suspended in linseed or other oil. Slower to dry than latex, it is more durable and requires renewing less often. Any paint's life span depends on temperature extremes, wind, humidity and sun exposure. Generally, when properly applied, latex paint will last three or four years, while oil or alkyd paint will last seven or eight years.

Alkyd, latex and oil paints are specially formulated for use on masonry surfaces. Properly applied, all will last three to five years. Powdered portland-cement paints for masonry are less expensive but cannot be painted over with a resin-based product. When latex or alkyd paint is applied to a concrete floor outdoors, where traffic is limited, it can be expected to last about a year before repainting is necessary.

FOUNDATION See Concrete

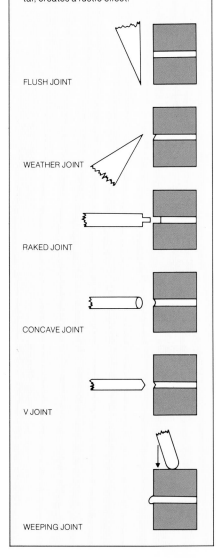

MORTAR JOINTS

As soon as the mortar joints in a masonry structure have hardened to a consistency that will retain a thumbprint, the joints can be shaped into final form. Finishing is not done just for esthetic reasons; the smooth, tightly compacted surface that results from shaping the mortar makes it more water and weather resistant.

After scraping off excess mortar from the joints with a trowel, shape the joints, vertical ones first. If your prime concern is waterproofing, choose a flush, weather or concave joint. A flush joint, made by troweling the mortar even with the face of the masonry, is the only style that creates no shadow. A weather joint, formed by troweling out the top of the joint, is aptly named because it sheds water so well. One of the commonest joints, the concave, can be shaped to different depths by angling the end of a steel pipe slightly larger than the joint. A variation on the concave is the V joint, cut with a trowel or special tool.

A raked joint, which requires a square-cut implement to push back the mortar, is particularly good-looking but is susceptible to seepage. The so-called weeping or tapped joint, shaped by tapping on top of the masonry above to squeeze out mortar, creates a rustic effect.

FLUSH JOINT

WEATHER JOINT

RAKED JOINT

CONCAVE JOINT

V JOINT

WEEPING JOINT

Glass

Safety is an important consideration when you choose glass panels for outdoor use. Check your building code to see if it specifies a minimum glass strength. Some codes require safety glass made of two layers with plastic or wire sandwiched between. Other codes allow tempered plate glass.

PANELS. Clear-glass panels deflect wind from a terrace or swimming pool without obstructing the view or blocking the sun's warmth. Textured glass panels transmit light while maintaining privacy. Glass is such a fragile material that installation is usually left to professionals. Since glass is also costly, plan to use panels in stock sizes to reduce both initial cost and the expense of replacement. Make sure panel frames are strong enough to prevent wind damage.

BLOCKS. Transparent or translucent glass blocks, joined with mortar, are used in walls and screens. Blocks are made of two hollow sections sealed together; they come in 8-by-4-, 8-by-8- and 12-by-4-inch sizes. Glass blocks last indefinitely but are an expensive building material.

JOIST See Wood

LATH See Wood
LIGHTS See Wiring
LUMBER See Wood

Mortar

A mixture of portland cement, sand and water with a small amount of lime or fire clay added for plasticity, mortar is used to bond stone, brick or concrete block. Dry-mixed mortar, sold in 10-, 25- or 50-pound bags at hardware stores and building-supply outlets, contains the correct ingredients in the right proportions and is ready to be mixed with water. Convenient for small jobs, it is costly for extensive work. Masonry cement, a premixed combination of cement and lime to which you add sand as well as water, is available in 70- and 80-pound bags.

A good all-purpose mix for garden masonry consists of 1 part portland cement, 1 part hydrated lime and 6 parts builder's sand. Stonework and retaining walls that are in contact with earth require a richer formula: 1 part portland cement, 3 parts sand and ¼ part hydrated lime or fire clay. With stone, use fire clay since lime causes discoloration.

Mix mortar in small batches to prevent premature drying. Using a wheelbarrow, wooden box or just a square of plywood, mix the dry ingredients with a hoe. Add water gradually, blending it in until the mixture has a buttery consistency and slips cleanly from the hoe. Use the mix within an hour, adding small amounts of water and remixing if the mortar begins to harden.

NAILS See Fasteners

OUTDOOR CARPETING See Carpeting, Outdoor

PAINT See Finishes
PANELS See Aluminum, Asbestos, Glass, Plastic, Screening
PAVING See Asphalt, Brick, Concrete, Soil Cement, Stone, Tile, Wood

Plastic

Because it is impervious to rot or corrosion, plastic is a useful, versatile garden-construction material. It appears in flat, corrugated or ridged panels, woven shade or insect screening, rigid pool molds, flexible sheets used to line pools and planters and to keep weeds out of walks, and in water and drainpipes.

SCREENS. Plastic shade screening, made of woven fibers, admits varying amounts of light depending on the tightness of the mesh. It is available in many colors and is simply cut to size and stapled to a wooden frame.

POOL LINERS. Rigid plastic pool molds, made in many shapes and sizes, are strong, rotproof fabrications that can be set directly into the ground. Less expensive are pool liners of flexible polyvinyl chloride (PVC) reinforced with nylon. Flexible sheets of plastic are also used to underlay walks or loose brick and gravel to discourage weeds.

PANELS. The most common use of plastic in garden construction is in the panels that are built into overhead or fence frames. Plastic panels can be selected to provide whatever degree of shade is desired. Such panels are available in sizes from 24 to 50 inches wide and in 8-, 10- or 12-foot lengths. There are many colors and degrees of transparency, ranging from nearly clear to opaque. The light colors, which reflect heat, are more commonly used in warm climates. Corrugations and ridges give plastic added strength.

Plastic panels can be secured to a wooden framework overhead or in a fence with an aluminum-twist nail driven through a neoprene washer. The washer helps to prevent cracking of the plastic as the nail is driven. Space the nails about a foot apart. If you use corrugated panels, drive nails through the crowns, not the valleys. Plastic panels can be cut with a fine-toothed handsaw or power-driven carborundum disc.

PIPES. Plastic pipe (pages 126, 149) has largely replaced copper or galvanized iron pipe in garden sprinkler and drainage systems because it is more economical and easier to install. Waterproof joints can be made simply by brushing a solvent on the end of a pipe and inserting it into a connector. But check your local building code; there may be restrictions on certain types or applications of plastic pipes.

PLYWOOD See Wood
POSTS See Wood
PRESERVATIVES See Wood Preservatives

Reed and bamboo

Woven into mats, stalks of reed and bamboo both provide overhead shade at low cost. They are easy to handle, needing only a light supporting framework to make a dappled shade pattern.

Woven reed is sold at plant nurseries and garden-supply stores in 25-foot rolls, 76 inches wide. It is held together with wire that can be cut and retwisted at any point. Either galvanized nails or 1-inch staples can be used to attach woven reed to a framework.

Woven bamboo, used indoors to shade screened porches, comes in rolls 3 to 12 feet wide and 6 feet long. There are two grades of bamboo—split and matchstick. Split bamboo is coarser and less regular than matchstick; it is also stronger. Matchstick is more flexible and easier to fix to an overhead frame.

For a simple cover to shade a terrace, a roll of reed or bamboo matting needs no more support than a frame of 2-by-4s, but exposed cut ends should be covered with wood molding.

Reed and bamboo can also be used in fence sections as a windbreak. Treated with a wood preservative, the matting will last several seasons but it is so inexpensive that most gardeners who use it replace it each year.

ROOFING See Aluminum, Canvas, Plastic, Reed and Bamboo, Screening, Wood

Sand

Grains of rock less than $\frac{1}{12}$ inch in diameter, sand is one of the basic components of concrete, mortar and stucco. Brick or flagstone terraces and walks are often laid without mortar on beds of sand 2 or more inches deep.

In concrete, a coarse, gritty, dry sand with particles ranging up to $\frac{1}{16}$ inch in diameter is best; this is often called builder's sand. Masonry sand consists of finer particles more uniformly sized and is used in mortar and stucco.

Any sand used in concrete, mortar or stucco must be clean. To check, put about 2 inches of sand in a quart jar filled with water and shake it. Let the jar stand overnight. If the layer of silt that forms is more than $\frac{1}{8}$ inch thick, the sand is too dirty to use. Never use beach sand in construction; its salt content prevents proper curing and bonding, and its sharp angular edges have been smoothed by the surf. You can tell so-called sharp sand, the kind you need, by rubbing a pinch near your ear. It should have a rasping noise.

Sand is available in 50- and 60-pound bags for small jobs, or, at lower cost, by the cubic yard. Store sand where it will stay dry; damp sand may upset your mixing calculations.

Screening

Woven screening made of wire or plastic filaments permits good ventilation while it shuts out insects. Though only special shade screens give controlled shade, any screening helps to reduce the glare of the sun.

Screening made of bronze, copper, plastic or aluminum has a long life expectancy if given reasonable care. Galvanized steel screening is strong and less expensive, but in time will require painting to prevent corrosion.

Where visibility is important, the thin strands of steel, bronze or copper screening give the best view. An occasional coat of varnish will prevent staining by bronze or copper. Plastic and aluminum filaments are thicker but they need no maintenance other than washing, though aluminum will be corroded by salt spray near oceans.

Wire screening comes in rolls from 16 to 72 inches wide, but the broader widths, 48 and 72 inches, are difficult to stretch taut before fastening.

Roof screening is simply stretched over a wood framework, stapled in place and further secured by narrow strips of wood nailed around the edges. Wall screening can be secured the same way, or you can use a special screen molding. For the latter, $\frac{3}{4}$-by-$1\frac{3}{4}$-inch lumber is partially cut along one edge so a thin strip can be removed, leaving a shallow recess. The screening is then stapled or nailed in this recess and the strip that was removed is replaced.

SCREWS See Fasteners
SLAT See Wood

Soil cement

Only ordinary garden soil and portland cement are used to make soil cement. This material provides a low-cost way to make hard paving that is appropriate for informal paths, parking areas, even terraces. The final surface, however, is more similar to hard-packed earth than to concrete.

A sandy soil is needed to create good soil cement; clay soil will not harden satisfactorily. To test your soil to see if it will suffice, mix small samples in various ratios; from 1 part cement to 6 parts soil, up to 1 part cement to 10 parts soil. Stir in water until a mixture squeezed in your hand will hold fingermarks but not drip. Put the mixture into a makeshift mold, a tin can or plastic cup, and let it harden for a week. Then remove the soil cement from the mold and check its hardness.

If your soil is suitable, grade the area to be paved, for good drainage, and install wood strips to prevent edge crumbling. Break up the soil to a depth of 4 to 6 inches and take out any rocks or plant debris. Mix about 9 parts soil to 1 part dry cement, dumping the cement into small piles and mixing it in. Compact the mixture with a lawn roller. Sprinkle with fine mist as long as the water is absorbed. When the surface is almost dry, sprinkle and roll again. Continue light sprinklings as long as the surface absorbs water, usually four or five days.

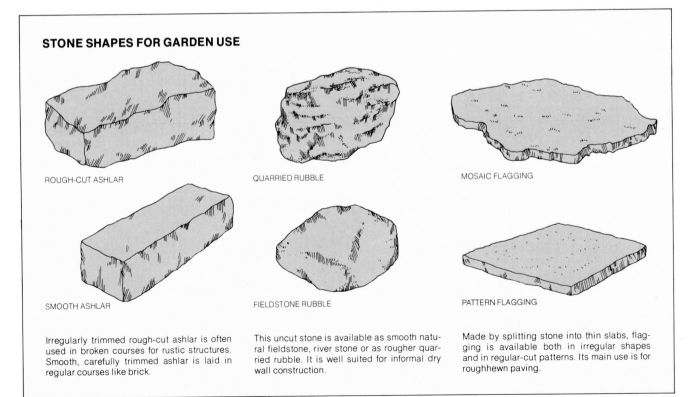

STONE SHAPES FOR GARDEN USE

ROUGH-CUT ASHLAR

QUARRIED RUBBLE

MOSAIC FLAGGING

SMOOTH ASHLAR

FIELDSTONE RUBBLE

PATTERN FLAGGING

Irregularly trimmed rough-cut ashlar is often used in broken courses for rustic structures. Smooth, carefully trimmed ashlar is laid in regular courses like brick.

This uncut stone is available as smooth natural fieldstone, river stone or as rougher quarried rubble. It is well suited for informal dry wall construction.

Made by splitting stone into thin slabs, flagging is available both in irregular shapes and in regular-cut patterns. Its main use is for roughhewn paving.

Sprinkler hardware

Pipes, heads and valves are the main components of an underground sprinkling system. Various fittings join the pipes to each other and to the heads that deliver the spray. Valves regulate the water supply at its source and, sometimes, at each sprinkler head.

Sprinkling-system pipes can be made of galvanized iron, semirigid PVC (polyvinyl chloride) plastic piping, or flexible polyethylene plastic piping.

Galvanized iron is the most difficult to install; special tools are needed to work with it. In time, internal corrosion may restrict the water's flow and make the system less efficient. But galvanized iron is not likely to be damaged by heat, rodents, freezing or wayward garden tools. In a high-pressure system galvanized iron is safer than polyethylene, which may burst, or PVC, which may leak at the joints. Iron pipes hold up well under the vibration of impulse-type spray heads.

Semirigid PVC pipe is available in lengths up to 20 feet that are easily cut with a hack saw. Fittings are attached with a solvent. Flexible polyethylene piping comes in lengths from 100 to 1,000 feet. Metal couplers and clamps join fittings and lengths of pipe. Either kind of plastic is less expensive than iron and easier to install. Plastic pipe does not corrode and it carries more water than steel pipe of the same size, since there is less internal friction.

Stationary and pop-up sprinkling heads are available. The former remain flush with the ground; the latter are lifted by water pressure when the water is on and drop back down when the water is turned off. Pop-up heads are more expensive than stationary heads and require higher water pressure but they water larger areas.

Most spray heads cover a circular area or some segment of one—three-quarter, half or quarter circles. A special type of head sprays rectangular or square areas; these overlap less than heads with circular patterns. Rotating impulse-type sprinklers throw bursts of water higher and farther, an advantage in sprinkling shrubbery or other tall plants. They are mounted above the ground and need high water pressure.

A variety of valves and timers are available to permit either manual or automatic control of the watering cycle.

STAIN See Finishes

Stone

Available in pebble-like gravel and boulder-sized chunks, in consistencies ranging from porous sandstone to tightly compacted granite, stones never look out of place in a garden. Stones can be used to pave a patio or terrace, to build a wall or rock garden, or simply as attractive ground covers. Their weight can make them difficult to work with, but once in place they are sturdy and virtually maintenance-free.

STONE SHAPES. Stones are sold in three forms: rubble, ashlar and flagging. Rubble is rough, uncut stone, quarried or taken from river and field. Large pieces of rubble—6 to 18 inches in diameter—are commonly used to build dry walls.

Smaller sizes of rubble stone, referred to as loose aggregates, include gravel, pulverized rock and crushed rock. They are used primarily as paving material. Gravel consists of naturally rounded pebbles from ¼ inch in diameter to an inch or more. It is often used as a drainage bed, but also provides a durable surface by itself.

Crushed rock, also called quarry stone, is man-made from larger rocks. The fragments range in size from ¼ of an inch to 1½ inches. Its sharp facets interlock tightly, making it the most stable of the loose aggregates.

Dustlike pulverized rock is the smallest aggregate. It is available as red rock, dolomite, decomposed granite or crushed brick, and generally is applied in two 3-inch layers, each moistened and compacted.

Ashlar stones are trimmed on all sides. Smooth or dressed ashlar stones are laid in regular courses like bricks and concrete blocks. Rough-cut ashlar stones are laid in irregular courses. Ashlar is available in common brick sizes (7½ to 8 inches long, 2¼ inches thick and 3¼ to 3½ inches wide) as well as in lengths up to 4 feet and heights up to 8 inches.

Flagging, or flagstone, is made by splitting stone into thin slabs. Thicknesses vary from approximately ½ inch to 2 inches; sizes range from 6 or 8 inches to 2 feet or more on a side. Used mostly for paving, flagging can be laid in regular patterns or irregular mosaics, on a bed of sand or on a concrete base.

VARIETIES OF STONE. All of these shapes—rubble, ashlar and flagging—are available in various kinds of stone; granite, limestone, slate, marble, bluestone and sandstone are the varieties that are most commonly used in garden construction.

Granite is hard and nonporous. It is difficult to cut and relatively expensive. Common granite is grayish, but it is often available in pink, white and green in textures from fine to coarse.

Limestone is not as hard as granite, but is strong enough to be used for most garden construction, including paving (it can support at least 60 tons per square foot). Limestone is porous and absorbs water quickly; it is a favorite for rock-garden construction. Limestone varies in color from dark gray and green to cream and off-white. It is chalky and easily cut.

Slate is hard and nonporous. It is naturally stratified and thus can be easily split into flagstones. It is available in shades of black, green and gray.

Marble is hard enough for many garden uses. Sold as smooth-cut ashlar, it is one of the most expensive construction materials, but it is also available in less costly chip form, used for gravel-type walks and pathways. Most marble is cream or pinkish white, but many other colors are available, from black to green to purple, depending on where the stone was quarried.

Bluestone is available in many colors besides blue, including pink, cream and red. Its rough surface is often used where nonskid paving is required.

Despite its misleading name, sandstone is nearly as strong as limestone. It is made up of sandy material (usually quartz) bonded by a natural cement such as silica. Its color ranges from yellow and white to buff and dark brown.

BUYING STONE. Flagging is sold by the square foot, rubble and ashlar by the cubic yard. To determine the amount of flagging needed for a paving job, measure the area and add an additional 10 per cent for breakage and replacement. To determine how much rubble or ashlar you need, multiply the length of the area to be surfaced by its width (in feet) by the desired depth (in a fraction of a foot), then divide that number by 27 (the number of cubic feet in a cubic yard). Use the same formula to compute the amount of material needed for a wall, substituting height for depth.

INSTALLING STONE. Paving stones are laid on a base of soil, sand or concrete. In areas of stable soil, the stones are laid out on the lawn in a pattern and their outlines marked with a shovel. Then they are removed one by one, the sod is removed to the depth of the stone or slightly less, and the stones are replaced.

Stones can be laid on a base of sand as shallow as 2 inches in mild climates;

up to 6 inches is advisable where severe freezing is common. Like bricks, paving stones are set on the sand and additional sand is brushed across them to fill the joints. Stones at least 2 inches thick are desirable to prevent cracking.

Stones as thin as ½ inch can be mortared to a poured concrete base. When the mortar has set, the joints can be filled with sand or grout.

Stones used in walls can be set dry or in mortar. The weight of the stones and their interlocking facets hold a dry wall together. A dry wall can be set directly on the ground or on a 6-inch layer of gravel. The stones are tilted inward to give the wall greater stability; bonding stones running the full width of the wall at intervals will add strength.

Mortared stone walls generally are set on concrete footings. The mortar mix that bonds the stones should be relatively thick so it will not seep out of the irregular joints.

Tools needed for working with stones include a trowel, mason's chisel, stonemason's hammer, shovel, hoe and level. A rake is needed to spread loose aggregates. Wear protective goggles when cutting stones.

Stucco

For durability and appearance, a layer of concrete called stucco is troweled over the exterior of wood or masonry structures. Stucco mortar is made of sand, portland cement and lime, differing from bricklaying mortar only in the smaller lime content. A basic stucco recipe, enough to cover about 24 square feet, consists of 200 pounds of builder's sand, 47 pounds of portland cement, 12 pounds of lime and 6 gallons of water.

Stucco is generally applied in three layers over metal lath. The first layer, the scratch coat, is ¼ to ⅜ inch thick. It is applied to the lath and is scored so the second layer, also ⅜ inch thick, will adhere. The final coat, about ⅛ inch thick, is the cosmetic coat that can be textured as desired. Tinted stucco cement is available in several colors for use in the finish coat. Stucco can also be painted with masonry paint.

Special tools needed for stuccoing include steel and wood trowels, a mortar board, a long wire brush, plus a hoe and wheelbarrow for mixing. Other materials used include metal flashing, metal lath, wood furring strips, building paper and nails.

If you mix and apply stucco, wear a long-sleeved shirt, gloves and goggles; the lime in the mix can irritate unprotected skin and eyes.

Tile

Made of hard-fired clay, tile is among the most durable of construction materials. Tile is used to make outdoor pavers, pipes for drainage systems and hollow blocks for walls.

DRAINAGE TILES. To divert water from a damp area, use red drainage tiles. These are cylindrical in shape, 4 to 6 inches in diameter and 1 foot long. They are placed end to end, unmortared, just below the drainage level of the soil and are covered with roofing felt or roofing paper, then with layers of gravel and sand in which excess water can disperse.

WALL TILE. The block-shaped hollow tile used in building walls can also be used to make ornamental planters. It is commonly available in 8-by-8, 4-by-16 and 8-by-16-inch face sizes, in thicknesses of 4, 6, 8, 10 and 12 inches. The glazed finish can be a variety of colors.

PAVING TILE. Unglazed patio, quarry and mosiac tile are used as pavers; they have a slightly textured surface to make them safe underfoot.

Patio tile is ¾ to ⅞ inch thick and comes in irregular sizes about 6-by-6, 6-by-12 and 12-by-12 inches, in shades of red and buff.

Quarry tile is more regular in shape (and more expensive) than patio tile. Its edges form precise right angles, so a smoother surface is possible than with patio tile, which has rounded edges. Quarry tile is available in many colors

---

LUMBER LENGTHS FOR DECKS AND OVERHEAD SUPPORTS

When designing a framework and calculating lumber needs for a garden deck or shelter, your first considerations should be structural soundness and safety. In general, flooring must be able to support a minimum of 50 pounds per square foot, including 10 pounds of dead weight in the structure itself. Roofing must support at least 30 pounds per square foot, possibly more where snowfall is heavy.

Post lengths and beam spans are the easiest to calculate. As a rule of thumb, a 4-by-4-inch post 8 feet long or less will support anything up to 8,000 pounds. But as post length increases, so do bending forces, reducing the weight that the post can carry. So a 4-by-4 post will support only 2,600 pounds if it is 14 feet long. A 4-by-6-inch post up to 8 feet long will carry 14,000 pounds.

The distance a beam can span is determined by its width: a 4-by-4 can span 4 feet, a 4-by-6 can span 6 feet, on up to a 4-by-12, which can span 12 feet. Beams should be placed with the wider side vertical.

For joists and rafters, the chart below gives the maximum length for each commonly used size of lumber, depending upon the spacing between boards. In each instance the length that is given equals the maximum span between supports. The greater the number of joists or rafters used in a given space, the longer each can be. It is often less expensive to space boards closer together and make them longer than to increase the size of lumber used, because the cost of a board is based more on its thickness than its length. For example, you may come out ahead by using 8-foot 2-by-4 rafters that are spaced 16 inches apart instead of 8-foot 2-by-6s that are spaced 32 inches apart. Spacing measurements are from the center of each board. As with beams, joists and rafters should be placed on edge.

MAXIMUM LENGTH OF LUMBER

Lumber Dimensions (in inches)	Spacing between Boards (center to center)		
	16 inches	24 inches	32 inches
For Joists:			
2 × 6	8 feet	6 feet	5 feet
2 × 8	10 feet	8 feet	7 feet
2 × 10	13 feet	10 feet	8 feet
For Rafters:			
2 × 4	8 feet	—	—
2 × 6	10 feet	10 feet	8 feet
2 × 8	16 feet	12 feet	12 feet
2 × 10	—	16 feet	16 feet

in sizes 4-by-4, 4-by-8, 6-by-6, 9-by-9 and 12-by-12 inches.

Mosaic tile, ¼ inch thick and 1 to 2 inches wide, is sold in a variety of designs, patterns and colors. It comes mounted on squares of paper or mesh, precisely spaced; a square of the small tiles can be laid in one operation, with the paper or mesh removed later.

The larger paving tiles can be laid in a smooth bed of sand 1 inch below grade, or they can be set with mortar or mastic on concrete, wood or brick.

Tile paving is luxurious; its cost is two or three times that of brick. Tile is also somewhat fragile and can be shattered if it is carelessly handled or improperly installed.

Tools needed for installing tile include a notched tile trowel, level, rule,

hoe, shovel, rake, mallet and wheelbarrow in which to mix mortar. Paving tiles are cut with a tile cutter, which is used to score a tile so it can be snapped like a piece of glass. Such cutters usually can be rented wherever tiles are sold. Curved cuts can be made with a mason's tool called a nipper.

Outdoor tile is set with a special mortar mix, sold in 20- to 50-pound sacks. When the mortar has cured for at least 48 hours, tile grout is used to fill the joints between the tiles, forming a watertight surface.

Wire fencing

For strong security fencing, chain-link and woven or welded-wire mesh are sold in patterns that are difficult to

climb, keeping small children and pets inside and garden pests out. Wire fencing is strong, long lasting and easy to maintain. Fencing made of aluminum wire is rustproof; that made of galvanized steel is rust-resistant. For a more decorative look, plastic-coated steel wire is made in a wide variety of colors including green and black.

Select woven or welded-wire fencing according to the size of the mesh openings, the height (up to 6 feet) and the gauge (diameter) of the wire. The usual gauges for home use are 11 to 15½, though heavier 6- to 9-gauge fencing is available. Wire fencing is sold in 50-foot rolls or in bales of 10 or 20 rods (a rod is 16½ feet). Some types of woven-wire fencing have crimps between the upright stays to compensate for expan-

LUMBER SIZES

Lumber is sold by thickness and width, in two-foot increments from 8 to 20 feet long. The thickness and width are given in the dimensions the board had when it was cut from the tree, or the "nominal" dimensions. When the board is milled, its size is reduced by the amount of rough wood cut off. As the sap and moisture dry out, shrinkage reduces its size even more. Thus, a nominal 2-by-4 is actually 1½ by 3½ inches; the actual size may be fractionally larger or smaller than that depending on the kind of wood. The accompa-

nying chart lists, in inches, the nominal size and actual dimensions (in parentheses) for several common lumber sizes.

If you need a board that is a full 1 inch or 2 inches thick, you can specify, but it will have to be milled to order and will be expensive. It is simpler to accept wood in the size it actually comes in, making measurements for your project accordingly and ignoring the nominal sizes. If you want a size not stocked, say a 2-by-5, you usually can have it cut at the lumberyard from the next larger size.

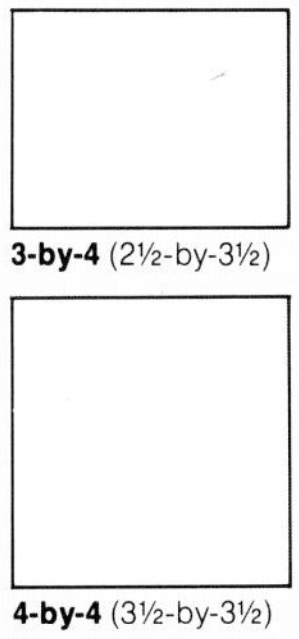

3-by-4 (2½-by-3½)

4-by-4 (3½-by-3½)

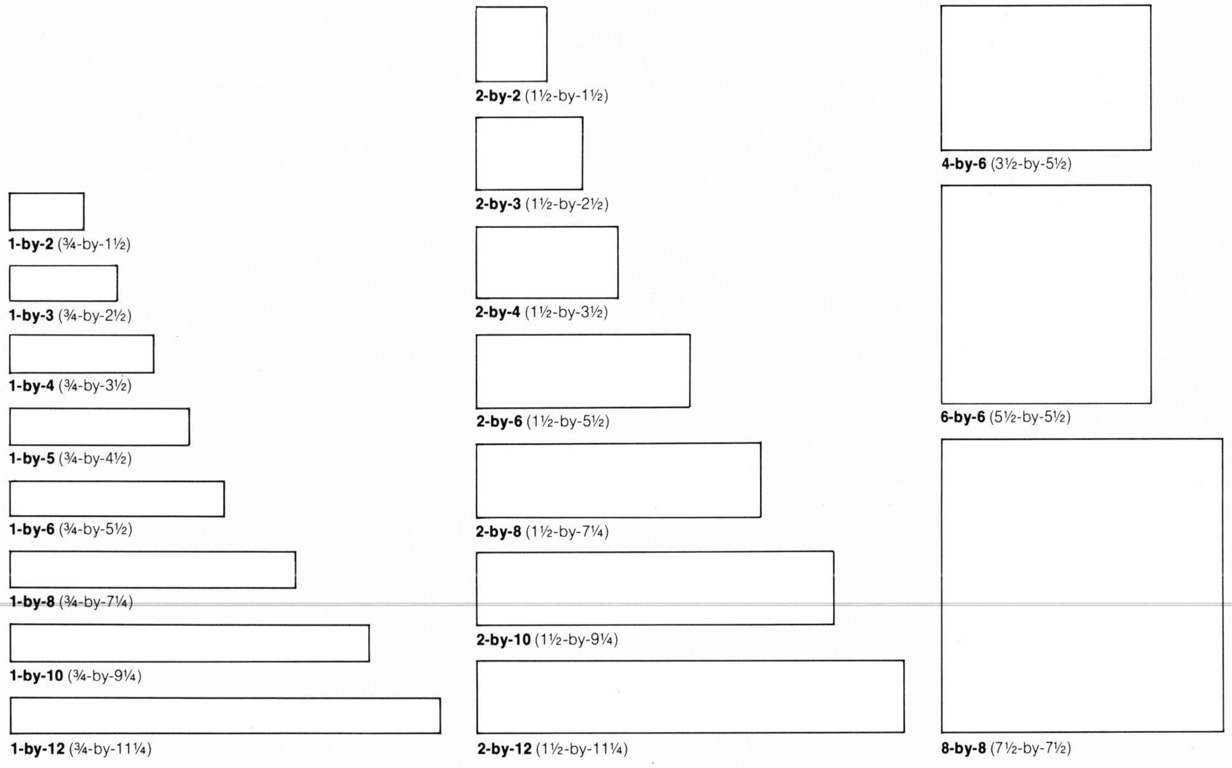

4-by-6 (3½-by-5½)

2-by-2 (1½-by-1½)

2-by-3 (1½-by-2½)

2-by-4 (1½-by-3½)

2-by-6 (1½-by-5½)

6-by-6 (5½-by-5½)

1-by-2 (¾-by-1½)

1-by-3 (¾-by-2½)

1-by-4 (¾-by-3½)

1-by-5 (¾-by-4½)

1-by-6 (¾-by-5½)

1-by-8 (¾-by-7¼)

2-by-8 (1½-by-7¼)

1-by-10 (¾-by-9¼)

2-by-10 (1½-by-9¼)

8-by-8 (7½-by-7½)

1-by-12 (¾-by-11¼)

2-by-12 (1½-by-11¼)

sion and contraction with seasonal temperature changes.

Chain-link fencing is sold by wire gauge (usually 9 or 11 for home use) and height (36, 42 and 48 inches). For enclosing swimming pools, chain-link fence 6 feet high is available. This fencing is generally sold in 50-foot rolls, complete with such hardware as steel posts, gates, hinges and top rails.

Installation of chain-link fencing is difficult and should be left in the hands of professionals. Lighter fencing, with wooden posts, can be installed satisfactorily by amateurs. Special tools needed include a posthole digger and a fence stretcher or block-and-tackle.

Metal picket fencing, sold in 36-, 42- and 48-inch rolls, needs no posts; it is simply pushed into the ground. In 16- and 22-inch heights, it is used primarily to identify the boundaries of flower beds and borders.

Wiring

Two kinds of systems are available to supply electricity to garden lights. One uses standard house current of 120 volts, the other a stepped-down 12 volts. Cables that carry 120 volts are potentially dangerous outdoors and must be protected with heavy weatherproof conduit.

Some electrical codes permit 120-volt plastic-sheathed cable to be buried directly in the ground. In other areas, the buried cable must be enclosed in metal tubing called conduit—either a thin-wall metal such as aluminum or a heavy-wall metal such as galvanized steel pipe. Usually, conduit must be buried at least 18 inches deep to reduce the chance of its being accidentally cut when the garden is spaded. It is wise when laying any cable to make a diagram showing where it is located, rather than to rely on memory.

In either case, the National Electrical Code specifies that 120-volt receptacles be connected to a device called a ground-fault interrupter (GFI). If hazardous current leakage occurs, the GFI immediately cuts off the electricity.

Low-voltage wiring, sheathed in waterproof plastic, carries only 12 volts; it is virtually shockproof and therefore far safer to handle, even when the current is on. The wire can safely be buried in a shallow 4- to 6-inch trench without extra protection but care must be taken not to cut it accidentally with garden tools. Kits for low-voltage wiring include a transformer that reduces the current from 120 volts to 12 volts, plus several lighting fixtures and up to 100 feet of wire.

Wood

Many kinds of softwoods are available for garden construction, so it is important to choose the type that will provide the appropriate strength and appearance for your project. Certain woods have characteristics that are particularly suited to specific garden uses, from simple planters to elaborate gazebos. While planning your project, however, keep in mind that some woods can be bought only in the regions where they are produced.

Softwoods such as Douglas fir and yellow pine, with their close-grained strength, are especially useful in heavy construction work. But cedar, redwood, spruce and white pine are slightly softer with a straighter, more predictable grain, and are therefore easier for the average gardener to saw and shape. Cedar, cypress and redwood are particularly decay-resistant and, along with spruce, more resistant to shrinking, swelling or warping than other types of softwoods.

The decay-resistant woods, especially redwood cut from the heartwood near the center of the tree, do not require treatment with preservative or paint, and may safely be sunk in the earth or otherwise exposed to constant moisture without danger of rotting. Other softwoods, however, should be treated with a wood preservative if they are to be used outdoors.

Softwoods may require periodic repairs and maintenance—painting and other refinishing—and even then they may in time deteriorate to the point where they must be replaced. The life expectancy of the wood will be determined in large part by where it is used and how well it is maintained.

WOOD PRODUCTS. Available wood products range from sawdust and bark chips to shingles and laths to boards, timbers and sheets of plywood, not to mention railroad ties and telephone poles. Most forms are classified according to their quality. A chart showing how lumber and plywood is graded is on the opposite page.

The smallest bits of wood—sawdust and chips—are used as mulches and ground covers. They tend to wash away in the rain and need a barrier to hold them in place. They are available at garden centers.

Buy lumber at a lumberyard or well-stocked building-materials store so you can be sure of finding the sizes and grades you need. Among the thin strips available are laths, 4- to 8-foot rough-cut strips 1½ inches wide and ⅜ inch thick. Lath is used for trellises to support climbing plants and for overheads and lath houses to protect tender or shade-loving plants.

For fences, ready-made pickets come in many shapes, from those with the traditional triangular tops to some with more intricate variations. Also used in fencing are grape stakes, 3- to 6-foot lengths of redwood that are about 2 inches square. Some gardeners split or saw grape stakes in half lengthwise to save wood.

Plywood can be used to build gates, fences, birdhouses and a host of other projects. It most commonly comes in 4- by 8-foot sheets ⁵⁄₁₆ to ¾ of an inch thick. Only exterior or marine-grade plywood should be used; otherwise the plies may come apart even if the structure is sealed against moisture.

For paving patios and paths, decay-resistant cedar, cypress or redwood blocks and round-cut sections about 4 inches thick can be placed randomly on a sand base. Useful for steps, edgings and low walls are railroad ties and landscape timbers, treated with a preservative so they will last many years.

Logs and rails are often available for building rustic furniture and fences. Used telephone poles, sometimes available from salvage dealers, are suitable for long retaining walls. Poles can be stacked lengthwise or cut into shorter segments to be placed vertically.

BUYING WOOD. Lumber is generally priced by quantity. Since boards come in many different sizes, a standard measure is achieved by converting the actual dimensions of the wood to an imaginary board foot 12 inches wide, 12 inches long and 1 inch thick. To compute board feet for any piece of lumber, simply multiply width and thickness in inches by length in feet, then divide by 12. When you buy lumber, note that the actual size of the wood you receive will be slightly less than the nominal size because the dimensions are reduced during the milling process. This difference may vary anywhere from ³⁄₁₆ to ½ inch. A 4-by-4-inch block of wood, for example, will be only 3½ by 3½ inches.

HANDLING. To keep boards from twisting and warping, store them flat on crosspieces so air will circulate around them. Keep lumber under cover to shield it from moisture.

Wood preservatives

Any wood that is to be used in garden construction, if it is not naturally rot-resistant, will benefit from treatment with wood preservative, a chemical that helps prevent decay and insect damage. A preservative properly applied will protect wood for 10 to 35 years, depending on soil and climate conditions. The best protection comes from the commercial application of the preservative under pressure; dip-treating at home (*page 15*) is economical but somewhat less effective.

Care must be taken in the selection and use of preservatives. Some are toxic to plants and hazardous to the person who applies them.

The oldest commonly used preservative is creosote, which leaves a dark, unpaintable stain and is very toxic. Pentachlorophenol-based mixtures do not leave smell or stain, but they are also toxic to plant life; they should be used with care, especially near prized specimens. Copper sulfate, which is good on unseasoned wood, leaves a blue stain. Copper and zinc naphthenates are nontoxic and odorless, although copper naphthenate leaves a pale green stain.

Commercially pressure-treated wood is widely available and is recommended for garden-construction projects. You can also buy preservative solution in quart or gallon containers at building-supply stores and apply it yourself. The more preservative the wood absorbs, the better it will be protected. It is especially important that the freshly cut ends of lumber be soaked in preservative, since the end grain is very susceptible to rot damage.

Spraying preservative gives poor coverage, and it may irritate the eyes and damage nearby plants. Apply it with a brush or, best of all, fill a trough and soak the wood in it.

Wrought iron

A malleable, corrosion-resistant metal, wrought iron can be hammered and welded into gates, posts, railings and other garden ornaments that will easily outlast their builders. But true wrought iron has become rare, except possibly at antique dealers. Most modern ironwork is milled steel, subject to corrosion if it is not protected with regular applications of primer and paint.

Such ornamental ironwork, in prefabricated designs, is available from steel fabricators and garden shops. It can also be made to order, although the cost is high. Supporting posts are anchored in fresh concrete, cemented in holes drilled in existing masonry or anchored in flanges bolted to either wood or masonry.

GRADES OF GARDEN-CONSTRUCTION LUMBER

SOFTWOOD GRADES
(including such woods as cedar, cypress, fir, pine and spruce)

SELECT: For quality indoor furnishings.

A	Virtually flawless. Used in the finest cabinet and furniture work.
B	A high-appearance lumber with smooth sides and faces; may show infinitesimal blemishes.
C	Has minor defects that can be concealed with a coat of paint.
D	Has small, tight knots that can be concealed with paint.

COMMON: For general construction purposes.

No. 1	Warp-free, though it may contain any number of solid knots. Excellent for outdoor furniture.
No. 2	May have coarser defects such as loose knots, discoloration and checks. Good for general garden construction.
No. 3	Small knotholes, pitch, checks, even warpage. Inferior sections may have to be cut out.
No. 4	Low-cost, low-quality construction lumber with many knotholes and coarse blemishes. Adequate for informal fencing.
No. 5	Inferior lumber riddled with large knotholes and other major defects.

STRUCTURAL: Beams and posts graded according to strength.

Construction	Top-quality structural lumber.
Standard	Slight defects, although strength is similar to construction grade.
Utility	An inferior structural grade. May be unsatisfactory for some garden construction; should be used only where other structural members add support. Not recommended for fencing.
Economy	Poor quality structural material. Should be used only for bracing or wooden crates.

REDWOOD GRADES

Clear All-Heart	Superior quality. Highly decay resistant and free of knots. Primarily used for fine furniture.
Clear	High-quality wood. May show small knots and minor blemishes. Excellent for outdoor benches and tables.
Select Heart	High-strength, all-heart redwood. May contain slight defects such as torn grain and small, sound knots.
Construction Heart	Good, general-purpose commercial-grade lumber. Recommended for posts, decks and small garden projects. May contain some large, tight knots.
Select	Free of imperfections but less decay resistant than heart grades.
Construction Common	Good, all-purpose construction lumber. May contain sapwood, tight knots and discoloration.
Merchantable	Contains loose knots and knotholes. Heartwood and sapwood are both included in this economical grade.

EXTERIOR PLYWOOD GRADES

A-A Exterior	Smooth, paintable, premier quality. Used where the appearance of both sides of the panel is important.
A-B Exterior	Excellent for painted surfaces or for natural finishes where the appearance of one side is slightly less important than the other. Both sides are sanded smooth although the back of the panel may show tight knots.
A-C Exterior	For use where the appearance of only one side is crucial. Face will be smooth-finished but the reverse may show 1-inch knotholes, tight knots and other defects.
B-B Exterior	An outdoor utility panel with paintable surfaces for use where appearance is not important.
B-C Exterior	Reasonably smooth surface on the face; knotholes and limited splits on the reverse.
C-C	An industrial product for use where appearance is not a factor. Unsanded surfaces are rough and hard to paint.

Appendix

Picture credits

The sources for the illustrations in this book are shown below. Credits from left to right are separated by semicolons, from top to bottom by dashes. Cover—Tom Tracy. 4—Sarah Tanner. 6—Courtesy Victoria and Albert Museum, Crown Copyright, London. 8 through 16—Drawings by Kathy Rebeiz. 19—Marina Schinz. 20—Marina Schinz, designed by Paul Prentice. 21 through 27—Marina Schinz. 28—John Zimmerman. 31 through 42—Drawings by Kathy Rebeiz. 45—Tom Tracy, designed by Edward Hume. 46—Tom Tracy, designed by Martin Stoelzel. 47—Enrico Ferorelli, designed by Johnson, Johnson and Roy, Inc. 48, 49—Tom Tracy, designed by Martin Stoelzel. 50 through 53—Tom Tracy, designed by Galper Baldon Associates. 54—Enrico Ferorelli. 56 through 61—Drawings by Kathy Rebeiz. 63, 64, 65—Linda Bartlett. 66, 69—Drawings by Kathy Rebeiz. 70—Tom Tracy. 73 through 78—Drawings by Kathy Rebeiz. 81—Tom Tracy. 82, 83—Entheos, designed by Torzeski. 84, 85—John Zimmerman. 86—Tom Tracy, designed by Pearl Richlin. 87—Peter B. Kaplan. 88, 89—Tom Tracy, designed by Joseph Copp Jr. 90—John Zimmerman, designed by B. C. Designs. 92—Drawing by Kathy Rebeiz. 93—Drawing by John Drummond. 94 through 100—Drawings by Kathy Rebeiz. 103—John Zimmerman, designed by B. C. Designs, lighting consultant Alan Desser. 104, 105, 106—Tom Tracy, designed by Martin Stoelzel. 107—John Zimmerman, designed by B. C. Designs, lighting consultant Alan Desser. 108, 109—John Zimmerman, designed by Thomas Church. 110—Illustration by Nicholas Fasciano. 112 through 153—Artists for encyclopedia illustrations listed in alphabetical order: Adolph E. Brotman; John Drummond; Nicholas Fasciano; Great, Inc.; Joan S. McGurren; John Sagan; Ray Skibinski; Vicki Vebell; Whitman Studio, Inc.; except photographs on page 141—Ken Kay. 143—Map courtesy U.S. Weather Bureau.

Bibliography

Anderson, L. O., Heebink, T. B., and Oviatt, A. E., *Construction Guides for Exposed Wood Decks*. U.S. Dept. of Agriculture, 1972.

Aul, Henry B., *How to Build Garden Structures*. Sheridan House, 1950.

Bailey, Liberty Hyde, *Garden-Making*. The Macmillan Co., 1898.

Better Homes and Gardens, *Deck and Patio Projects You Can Build*. Meredith Corp., 1977.

Better Homes and Gardens, *Garden Ideas and Outdoor Living*. Meredith Corp., 1977.

Brann, Donald R., *Concrete Work Simplified*. Directions Simplified, Inc., 1974.

Brann, Donald R., *How to Build Outdoor Projects*. Directions Simplified, Inc., 1975.

Brett, William S., and Grant, Kay, *Small City Gardens*. Abelard-Schuman, London, 1967.

Brimer, John Burton, *Designs for Outdoor Living*. Doubleday and Co., Inc., 1959.

Brimer, John Burton, *Homeowner's Complete Outdoor Building Book*. Harper & Row, 1971.

Brooklyn Botanic Garden, *Gardening in Containers*. BBG, 1958.

Brooklyn Botanic Garden, *Handbook on Garden Construction*. BBG, 1964.

Church, Thomas, *Your Private World: A Study of Intimate Gardens*. Chronicle Books, 1969.

Clifford, Derek, *A History of Garden Design*, rev. ed. Frederick A. Praeger, Publishers, 1966.

Cruikshank, Allan D. and Helen G., *1001 Questions Answered About Birds*. Dodd, Mead and Co., 1960.

Daniels, George, ed., *Decks, Porches, and Patios*. Meredith Corp., 1974.

Day, Richard, *The Home Owner Handbook of Concrete and Masonry*. Bounty Books, 1974.

Day, Richard, *How to Build Patios and Decks*. Harper & Row, 1976.

Debaights, Jacques, *Swimming Pools*. Charles E. Tuttle, Co., Inc., 1973.

Derven, Ronald, and Nichols, Carol, *Book of Successful Swimming Pools*. Structures Publishing Co., 1976.

Dietz, Marjorie J., *Landscaping and the Small Garden*. Doubleday, 1970.

Durbahn, Walter E., *Fundamentals of Carpentry Tools, Materials and Practices*. American Technical Society, 1967.

Eckbo, Garrett, *The Art of Home Landscaping*. McGraw, 1956.

Edwardes, S. M., *Babur: Diarist and Despot*. A. M. Philpot, Ltd., London, 1975.

Farrington, Edward L., *The Gardener's Travel Book*. Oxford University Press, 1949.

Fields, Curtis P., *The Forgotten Art of Building a Stone Wall*. Yankee, Inc., 1971.

Foerster, Bernd, *Pattern and Texture*. School of Architecture, Rensselaer Polytechnic Institute, 1961.

Foley, Daniel J., *The Complete Book of Garden Ornaments, Complements and Accessories*. Crown Publishers, 1972.

Garland, Madge, *The Small Garden in the City*. George Braziller, 1974.

Givens, Harold, *Landscape It Yourself*. Harcourt, Brace, Jovanovich, Inc., 1977.

Harshbarger, Gretchen Fischer, *McCall's Garden Book*. Simon & Schuster, Inc., 1968.

Hawkins, Reginald R., and Abbe, Charles H., *Arbors and Trellises—Breezeways, Fences and Gates—Small Buildings*. D. Van Nostrand Co., Inc., 1951.

Hellyer, Arthur, *The Collingridge Guide to Your New Garden*, 4th rev. ed. The Hamlyn Publishing Group, Ltd., 1975.

Heritage, Bill, *The Lotus Book of Water Gardening*. The Hamlyn Publishing Group, Ltd., 1973.

Hudson Home Guides, *Decks & Patios*. Bantam/Hudson Idea Books, 1976.

Huff, Darrell, *How to Work With Concrete and Masonry*. Harper & Row, 1968.

Kalmbach, E. R., and McAtee, W. L., *Homes for Birds*. U.S. Dept. of the Interior, 1969.

Kramer, Jack, *Fences, Walls and Hedges for Privacy and Security*. Charles Scribner's Sons, 1975.

Kramer, Jack, *Gardening and Home Landscaping*. Harper & Row, 1971.

Kramer, Jack, *The Outdoor Garden Build-It Book*. Charles Scribner's Sons, 1977.

Kramer, Jack, *Planters*. Ballantine Books, 1977.

Martin, George A., ed., *Fences, Gates, and Bridges*. The Stephen Greene Press, 1974.

McElroy, Thomas P., Jr., *The New Handbook of Attracting Birds*. Alfred A. Knopf, 1970.

Minnesota Mining and Manufacturing Co., *The Home Pro Brick, Concrete and Stonework Guide*. Borden Publishing Co., 1975.

Nunn, Richard V., *Decks and Patios*. Oxmoor House, 1977.

Olin, Harold B., Schmidt, John L., and Lewis, Walter H., *Construction Principles, Materials and Methods*. The Institute of Financial Education and Interstate Printers and Publishers, Inc., 1975.

Organic Gardening and Farming, *Build It Better Yourself.* Rodale Press, Inc., 1977.

Ortho Books, *Container and Hanging Gardens.* Chevron Chemical Co., 1975.

Ortho Books, *Garden Construction Know-How.* Chevron Chemical Co., 1975.

Ortho Books, *Gardening Shortcuts.* Chevron Chemical Co., 1977.

Ortho Books, *Wood Projects for the Garden.* Chevron Chemical Co., 1976.

Philbin, Thomas, *The Practical Handbook of Patio and Outdoor Projects.* W. Foulsham & Co., Ltd., London, 1975.

Portland Cement Association, *Cement Mason's Guide to Building Concrete Walks, Drives, Patios, and Steps.* Portland Cement Association, 1971.

Ramsey, Charles George, and Sleeper, Harold Reeve, *Architectural Graphic Standards.* John Wiley & Sons, Inc., 1956.

Reader's Digest Association, *Complete Do-It-Yourself Manual.* RDA, 1972.

Reader's Digest Association, *Reader's Digest Practical Guide to Home Landscaping.* RDA, 1972.

Schuler, Stanley, *The Complete Terrace Book.* Macmillan Publishing Co., Inc., 1974.

Schuler, Stanley, *Gardening from the Ground Up.* The Macmillan Co., 1968.

Schuler, Stanley, *How to Build Fences, Gates and Walls.* Macmillan Publishing Co., Inc., 1976.

Schuler, Stanley, *Outdoor Lighting For Your Home.* D. Van Nostrand Co., Inc., 1962.

Schutz, Walter E., *How to Attract, House and Feed Birds.* Collier Books, 1970.

Simonds, John Ormsbee, *Landscape Architecture.* McGraw-Hill Book Co., Inc., 1961.

Smith, Alice Upham, *Patios, Terraces, Decks and Roof Gardens.* Hawthorn Books, Inc., 1969.

Stewart, Shan, *Planning and Building Your Patio.* Crown Publishers, 1954.

Stoffel, Robert J., *Do's and Don'ts of Home Landscape Design.* Hearthside Press, Inc., 1968.

Sunset Editors, *Garden Work Centers.* Lane Publishing Co., 1972.

Sunset Editors, *How to Build Decks.* Lane Publishing Co., 1976.

Sunset Editors, *How to Build Fences and Gates.* Lane Publishing Co., 1972.

Sunset Editors, *How to Build Walks, Walls and Patio Floors.* Lane Publishing Co., 1976.

Sunset Editors, *Outdoor Lighting.* Lane Publishing Co., 1971.

Terres, John K., *Songbirds in Your Garden.* Thomas Y. Crowell Co., 1953.

Thomas, G. L., Jr., *Garden Pools, Water-Lilies, and Goldfish.* D. Van Nostrand Co., Inc., 1958.

U.S. Dept. of the Army, *Concrete, Masonry and Brickwork.* Dover Publications, Inc., 1975.

Wagner, Willis H., *Modern Carpentry.* The Goodheart-Willcox Co., Inc., 1976.

Wakeling, Arthur, ed., *Garden Furniture, Barbecues and Fences.* The Home Craftsman Publishing Corp., 1953.

Acknowledgments

The index for this book was prepared by Anita R. Beckerman. For their help in the preparation of this book, the editors wish to thank the following: Adobe News, Los Lunas, N.M.; Henry E. Ahari, Staff Engineer, National Sand and Gravel Association, National Ready Mixed Concrete Association, Silver Spring, Md.; Pamela Allsebrook, California Redwood Association, San Francisco, Calif.; American Plywood Association, Tacoma, Wash.; American Wood Preservers Institute, McLean, Va.; Mai K. Arbegast, Berkeley, Calif.; Mr. and Mrs. Allen A. Atwood, Alexandria, Va.; Balcon, Inc., Customized Concrete Masonry and Concrete Products, Baltimore, Md.; Baltimore Concrete Block Corp., Baltimore, Md.; Fred Belden, Assistant Landscape Architect, The Colonial Williamsburg Foundation, Williamsburg, Va.; Mr. and Mrs. Gary Blatt, San Rafael, Calif.; Mr. and Mrs. Bert J. Blum, Encino, Calif.; Mrs. Roger W. Brett, Rancho Sante Fe, Calif.; Brick Institute of America, McLean, Va.; California Redwood Association, San Francisco, Calif.; Canvas Products Association International, St. Paul, Minn.; Charles Carr, President, Miniature Lighting Products Co., Inc., Port Richey, Fla.; Chain Link Fence Manufacturers Institute, Washington, D.C.; Beth Cocanougher, Scottsdale, Ariz.; Joseph Copp Jr., Los Angeles, Calif.; Alan Desser, Los Angeles, Calif.; Mrs. Theodore G. Driscoll, Alexandria, Va.; Dr. T. R. Dudley, Research Botanist, U.S. National Arboretum, Washington, D.C.; Dr. and Mrs. Samuel Ellsworth, Alexandria, Va.; Dr. and Mrs. Morley Engelson, Beverly Hills, Calif.; Marie Froug, Alexandria, Va.; Mr. Sid Galper, Galper Baldon Associates, Venice, Calif.; Mrs. D. M. Gardner, Western Wood Products Association, Portland, Ore.; Gerald L. Garner, San Diego, Calif.; Barbara Goldenberg, B. C. Designs, Los Angeles, Calif.; Grace Hall, Thomas Church and Associates, San Francisco, Calif.; John and Mary Margaret Hansen, Houston, Tex.; Henry and Skip Hathaway, Los Angeles, Calif.; The Hechinger Company, Va.; Mr. and Mrs. R. H. Hellman, Santa Barbara, Calif.; Sandra Hinson, Orlando, Fla.; Edward Hume, Edward Hume and Associates, Los Angeles, Calif.; Janet Huseby, Berkeley, Calif.; Carl Johnson, Johnson, Johnson and Roy, Inc., Ann Arbor, Mich.; Alfred S. Keller, Pacific Palisades, Calif.; William F. Kelsey, Kelsey-Kane Lighting Mfg. Co., Fort Lauderdale, Fla.; Patricia O. LaLand, The Colonial Williamsburg Foundation, Williamsburg, Va.; Victor G. Link, Director, Soil Survey Operations Division, U.S. Dept. of Agriculture, Washington, D.C.; Bernie Mallon, Cushwa Brick and Building Supply Co., Springfield, Va.; Milliken Residence, Traverse City, Mich.; Mr. Bahram Nahidian, Washington, D.C.; National Concrete Masonry Association, McLean, Va.; Mr. Abdel Rahman Osman, Librarian, The Islamic Center, Washington, D.C.; Donald H. Parker, Director, Landscape Architecture, The Colonial Williamsburg Foundation, Williamsburg, Va.; J. Liddon Pennock Jr., Meadowbrook Farm Greenhouse, Meadowbrook, Pa.; Carol Peress, Alexandria, Va.; Gradie Philipp, Alexandria, Va.; Mr. and Mrs. Dean L. Phillips, Studio City, Calif.; Portland Cement Association, Skokie, Ill.; Paul Prentice, Alexandria, Va.; Sally Reath, Devon, Pa.; Pearl April Richlin, Sherman Oaks, Calif.; Jane Rieker, Boynton Beach, Fla.; Mr. J. W. Schwartz, Staff Specialist, Soil, Water and Air Sciences, U.S. Dept. of Agriculture, Beltsville, Md.; William Pete Sears, Santa Barbara, Calif.; Martin Stoelzel, San Rafael, Calif.; Mrs. Walter E. Thwing, Southbury, Conn.; Torzeski, San Diego, Calif.; Sid Tucker, Mill-to-You, Inc., Forestville, Md.; Mr. and Mrs. Thomas Tuttle, Alexandria, Va.; Emmat Walker, Turf Management, Washington, D.C.; Gloria Watson, Alexandria, Va.; West Coast Lumber Inspection Bureau, Portland, Ore.; Western Wood Products, Portland, Ore.; Mr. and Mrs. Q. T. Wiles, Los Angeles, Calif.; Alfred T. Wilkes, Los Angeles, Calif.; Patricia Young, California Redwood Association, San Francisco, Calif.

Index

Numerals in italics indicate an illustration of the subject mentioned.